A Love Relationship By Design

Passion, Perception and Purpose
…with a Touch of Poetry

by Stephen Wright

"A Love Relationship by Design" ©
by Stephen Wright
Copyright © 2016

All rights to this book are strictly reserved, which includes the right to reproduce this book or portions thereof in any form whatsoever without the written permission of the publisher as provided by the U.S. Copyright Law.

For information regarding copyright please contact:

Smooth Sailing Press. LLC
Attn: Publisher
PO Box 1707
Conroe, TX 77305

(281) 826-4026
www.smoothsailingpress.com

SAN: 257-2680

ISBN: 978-1-61899-017-4

Abridged 2016

Printed in the USA

A Love Relationship

By Design

Stephen Wright

DEDICATION

To my parents, Reverend Harry and Dolly Wright, Sr., who raised me in the church and have been my biggest supporters.

I also want to dedicate this book to my son Steven who is an intelligent and great kid. He is also my prayer partner and often encourages me to read more which has made me a better man.

This book is also to help prepare him to someday enjoy marital bliss. It is designed to give a view of how God intended us to love in a man to woman relationship and for him to respect, treasure and honor all women, starting with his mother.

A Love Relationship by Design

Table of Contents

Introduction 3

The Original Design 5

The Head and His Helper 9

The Perfect Compliment 12

The Fall and Rise of a Leader 18

How We Fit... 25

Revising the Thought Process 34

In the Beginning There Was Passion 47

Understanding Affections 53

Physical Touch... 55

Passionate Intimacy 58

Compliments, Notes and Coupons 68

A Word in Season 72

Bearing Each Other's Burden 75

Man's Passion for His Wife 80

Giving Sacrificially 82

Perception and How To Change It 84

Changing our Perception 92

A Love Relationship by Design

The Hunter	95
Provision	104
Setting the Standards	110
Human Requirements	116
An Unequal Yoke Drives Perception	124
Change Management	127
Checks and Balances	136
Actions and Reactions	138
Communication Eliminates Perception	142
Purpose	148
Purpose of Union	150
Man as Priest	154
Purpose of a Helpmate	157
Purpose of a Cultivator	163
Identifying God's Purpose	167
The Effect of Neglected Purpose	170
Servants of Each Other	173
Author Biography	177

A Love Relationship by Design

Introduction

The human relationship is one of God's most vital creations. His creative design was meant, in essence, to bring about fullness. It is one of the many ways God communicates with us in human form. The way we treat others, and they us, should display the very heart of our creator. Male and female are the same because both have the ability to give and receive love, although how they express it and to what extent may differ. We all, at some point, have experienced feelings of love, but not everyone has been loved correctly or understood how to truly love someone the way God intended. Effectively loving someone means to love them down to their soul, beyond their faults and failures— In order to truly love, we must examine God's original intent for man and woman. Truly loving someone is not just a mere reflection of you, but a reflection of God, the One who first loved you.

A Love Relationship by Design

A Love Relationship by Design

The Original Design

God said, *"Let us make man in Our image."* Genesis 1:26 (NKJV). The Apostle John defines God as a spirit in John 4:24, which says man is, in part, a spiritual being, living in a fleshly body, but beyond that, God's presence, His personality and His character were imparted into humanity. The very first intimate relationship was between God and man It symbolized the life of humanity birth from the spirit of God.

God spoke and whatever He said came to pass, and likewise Adam named the animals and they were called what he named them. God created and gave man the ability to procreate. In this, we see the resemblance of God in man. The use of the word "our" confirms what we know as the "triune," meaning the God head: the Father, the Son and the Holy Spirit. The nature and composition of man is both spiritual and physical. The physical being our "outer core" made from the dust of the ground. This outer core is fallible, and will return again to the dust. The inner man is spiritual; we are spiritual beings living a natural experience. God, forming man from the dust of the ground, shows His sense of humor. When we get dust in our home we vacuum it up and when dust gets on our car we wash it off, but in the hands of God this useless sediment is transformed into a glorious masterpiece. On one hand, mankind is human, created from the dust of the earth, and requires nourishment such as food, water, attention, conversation, socialization, and reciprocal affection. On the other hand, man is the "breath" of God, spiritual in nature. His soul cannot live without God's existence. He needs the word of life, communication and fellowship with God, and certainly His Spirit or presence for direction. Together flesh and spirit make a whole man. Each part is vital in sustaining the balance of the fully functioning earth man. When either is absent, he is not complete.

> Genesis 2:18 (NKJV) God said, *"It is not good that the man should be alone."*

According to Clark's Commentary, the Hebrew word for *alone* means "only himself" …I will make him a *helpmate*; a help, a counterpart of himself, one formed from him, and a perfect resemblance of his person. If the word be described literally, it signifies one like or as himself, standing opposite to or before him. This implies that the creation of woman was to be a perfect resemblance of the man, possessing neither inferiority nor superiority, but being in all things like and equal to him. "Adam Clark 1760 or 1762-1832." Note the previous section is from the Clarks Bible commentary and the original word used is help meet, which means to compliment the man. All the animals had companions

A Love Relationship by Design

but yet the prince of God creation was without one. In this application it is good to have someone to celebrate your victories and share comfort in your defeats.

"I will make him a helper comparable to him." Genesis 2:18b. (NKJV)

"Comparable," refers to custom tailored or custom fit to his need. Eve was "made to fit." The NIV uses the words "I will make a helper suitable for him." The Hebrew word for "helper" is *ezer* (pronounced "ay-zer"), According to R. David Freedman, the word *ezer* is a combination of two roots, meaning "to rescue/to save" and "strength".[For sake of argument they were slated to be a strong fit or suit. In a viable relationship, they are only strong as their ability to function in their role as a team. This was the second intimate relationship God formed. The woman was taken from the rib which is close to the heart. A relationship, that's if it was an intimate as intended would have prevented what would happen next. The fit was intended to be intimate. Intimate, according to Oxford dictionary, means "Closely acquainted; Private and personal." When our relationships are this way, it keeps the enemy from dividing and conquering. -A man seeking a mate must be careful, because every woman is not a suitable fit for just any man and vice versa. The word *"made"* is from the Hebrew word *"Asah,"* it is defined as *making from what already exists*. In this case, Eve was taken out of man, God's original creation, specifically the rib of Adam. Man and woman are of one body, so they are equals in that respect, both expressing ideas and opinions; let us call this, "duality".

A Love Relationship by Design

The Head and His Helper

As we consider that man and woman *are* of one body, it is important to note that with one body there can only be one head. God brings order to the family after the fall in the Garden. In Genesis 3:16b "Your desire *shall be* for your husband, And he shall rule over you." Man was created to function as the head and leader of his duality, his home. Headship is not about power, but about order and structure, it is a functioning role. God created Adam with purpose; in him, He defined masculine, designed and gifted with physical strengths, and survival and provisioning directives. He created Eve as feminine, a companion with the ability to multiply life and give strength. The nature of water is a counter balance to man. Everything about the woman highlights multiplication. She is a multitasked. She talks more, she analysis and looks into things, and her emotions are heightened.

God has once more made whole their duality by providing one half with outer strength, and the other with inner strength; and to each, a set of complementing purposes within those strengths. We can consider this wisdom further by taking a deeper look into its characteristics. A woman's emotional side is her strength; it makes her sensitive to other's needs.

However, emotions can also serve as a weakness if they govern decisions without rationalizing thoughts. Man's counter-balance is in his gift to analyze, rationalize, and provide practical perspective, without emotional interference. Although men will express some emotions, it is not nearly as expressive as women's; however, men can also make irrational decisions under emotional distress. It solely depends on the temperament of the person. However, men repress or internalize their emotions which can make insensitive to the needs of women.

> Ephesians 5:23a (NKJV) *"...for the husband is head of the wife, as also Christ is head of the church."*

The hierarchy in the family is God, man, woman and children. Today, too many men tend to avoid their role because they do not want the responsibility or accountability it carries. This is not to say a woman does not possess headship abilities because she most certainly does. She often fulfills this role when men become passive; however it is the plan of God for man to be the head of the wife. The woman is the "fetus male" or the "womb man" because of her ability to reproduce the seed of the man.

The man is significantly insufficient without the woman for she is able to do what he cannot on his own.

A Love Relationship by Design

She is the birth canal to all sustainable human existence and is the conduit. As a compliment to the male, she possesses the God given ability to reproduce man's vision, purpose, and aspirations. Unfortunately, she also has to ability to reproduce and multiply his ill deeds. And contrary to her nature, she can become his worst enemy. A disconnection in functionality can occur when the man or woman perform or act outside of their God ordained roles. A man or woman can imitate each other's role but they cannot operate in its fullness while being who they are not. This reversal of roles leads to a dysfunctional home, whereby the woman is head and the man is the helper. Regardless of who tries to be what, the man is held accountable by God. Today, our society, selfishness, upbringing, and alternative lifestyles have altered our view of mankind as God intended.

A Love Relationship by Design

The Perfect Compliment

As described by King Solomon in Proverbs 31, the woman is to be the *perfect complement to the man for Gods purpose..* Her characteristics are the **mirror** of his identity but most importantly, she is the classic portrait of the "perfect helpmate."

I used the word mirror above for two reasons. First, when you face a mirror and extend your hands it gives the appearance of touching your image. This is a symbolism to each other. Secondly, when you face this mirror, you can see an image of yourself. The Proverbs 31 woman, this "perfect helpmate" is the resemblance of the man and woman together in unity.

This phenomenal woman does not need to be coached; she knows what she has to do and is diligent in making sure it is done. She is described as being more precious than rubies… she is the refined Eve. The scripture writer's intent was to express her worth. The word rubies used in the original language also included pearls. In biblical times, as they are today, natural pearls were considered of great value. This meant, the phenomenal woman's worth far exceeded the value of diamonds, implying that not even the greatest of all known jewels could compare to her value. No nominal

A Love Relationship by Design

tag can be placed on her, because she is considered priceless. She is virtuous and exhibits moral excellence. Her character speaks for itself and she is identified by it. She treats her husband like a man of honor and brings good to him and not evil. He can safely trust his heart to her.

King Solomon also wrote that this perfect woman enjoys working with her mind and hands. She is like an entrepreneur that finds and researches what it takes to be successful at every task. In today's translation, this could mean many things. Amongst them, we can identify wisdoms such as 'stretching' the family's budget through wise purchases. The family's needs are her responsibility, thus she ensures all needs are met. When you think of the word "Helpmate" or the original word "help meet," it translates into one who helps. When a woman compliments the man by aiding to the success of the family, even by the saving of money, it helps make him a better man. Her wisdom contributes to him in the area of family needs. This is not something the woman has to be told or reminded of, but she naturally immerses herself into.

The old adage of 'Behind every good man is an even greater woman' comes to life within the Proverbs 31 woman, as her actions behind the scenes make her husband stand out, often doing the work but allowing him to take the credit. Realizing her tongue has a

A Love Relationship by Design

creative force for doing good or evil, to build up or tear down, the woman will build up her man with her words; knowing that they produce life. In this same way, the woman will speak to—and of—her children, helping in their mental and spiritual development.

She is a noble woman. She manages her household with wise standards and her children are a credit to their community.

She is what Adam would classify as "flesh of my flesh and bone of my bone, meaning she is the very essence of who he is . Family is very important to her and she is one with her husband.

How does a man recognize the perfect woman? How does one really know when a person has been sent by God? Because men are visual and can be distracted by what is apparent in physical appearance, they can have the right person and not know it. I am convinced that when she appears it will be recognizably evident based on her ability to connect and meet the needs to your purpose. Something about her will set her apart, however, man can possess his own blind shots. Those bias views and misconceptions of his Godly needs can cause him not to see her, because he is only looking from a natural window The question could be does he really know what he need? What was it that Jacob recognized in Rachel that made him both wait and work for her? He worked seven years and then offered to work another seven years. Rachel was not plain; there was nothing ordinary about her. She was characteristically unique. She was also consistent. She drew daily from the well. Jacob saw what she possessed and was willing to both, wait and work to acquire her.

When a man is willing to wait and work for a woman then she must possess value.

Ruth 4:11 says Rachel and Leah were builders of Israel. Jacob happened upon Rachel at the well and to him, it was love at first sight. In fact, he wept out of joy for a potential wife.

In the case of Boaz, he was a wealthy man and Ruth a poor widow, similar to Jacob with Rachel, he singled her out in this same way. In Ruth 3:10-11 Boaz speaks of two things that stand out. First, Ruth was "loyal" " and second, she was a "woman of worth."

When a man crosses path with a woman of this caliber, there is potential of a Godly mate;

"Protocol"

I know that pride
Comes before the fall
But I am not at all prideful
I am subject to your heart's protocol.
*What is the **modus operandi**?*

A Love Relationship by Design

The procedure- to which I pledge...I stand
I stand for Jesus Christ, I stand as a leader.
I stand as a faithful, one woman man.
I will campaign grass roots for your love.
I will be meticulous in my endeavor.
I will lobby to win your approval, and your smile.
My interest is to love you forever.
You hold a high office
in the love chamber of my Capitol Hill.
Put it into legislation, so I can sign the deal
to pass this much needed love bill.
You are witty, clever and smart.
You have a voice that is powerful yet meek.
So instead of using my executive powers
I choose to let you baby, "The people Speak."
Will you let me love you?
Will you allow me to give you much needed affection?
I will fight for just us --I stand for change.
I will take your heart in a whole new direction.
I pledge my allegiance to you always.
I will embrace the agenda of hope.
Equality in our pursuit of happiness
will be the theme of my presidential scope.
You are my first lady...with words of affirmation
I will hold you in high esteem.
When I am forced to make an executive decision,
I will consult you, the highest rank on my cabinet team.
I will bring you gifts, like rare fine chocolate from
Colombia
and hand knitted garments from Pakistan.
Whether we are together or on separate agendas,
you are my cooperative...
the continuity of God's companion plan.

A Love Relationship by Design

Let there be Acts of Service between you and I.
We are knitted by the fabric of life- we are community.
So I do solemnly promise to uphold and defend your honor
that you may enjoy this liberty.
If the Secretary of Defense issues a code red,
the highest terror alert
I am not at all afraid to love you with all my life.
Because I know your value…yes I know your worth.
Put it into legislation, call a special session,
stamp it with your seal of approval and let me sign the bill,
so I can carry out this much needed love deal.
If we have to spend quality time in a special session,
with verbal commitment into the night,
let's explore the dynamics with mutual interest
to make this love policy right.

A Love Relationship by Design

The Fall and Rise of a Leader

After sin was introduced in the Garden of Eden, Adam hid from God, yet God went looking for Adam because He knew that it was necessary for Adam to be the spiritual authority in his family[i]. When you read the scripture below, note that God did not go looking for Eve, but for Adam, because He gave Adam the instruction regarding the tree of knowledge.

> Genesis 3:9 (NKJV) *Then the LORD God called to Adam and said to him, "Where are you?"* First, God created man and then gave him a charge concerning the trees in the Garden of Eden. He then created the woman.

Note an mere observation from Genesis chapters two and three. Adam is vocal and chapter 2 but goes silent in chapter 3. Why did Adam go silent? Was it conflict, confidence, or merely co-existence issues? No matter the cause, what did exist was the lack of courage. During the serpent conversation with Eve, Adam was silent when he should have spoken, and Eve spoke when she should have referred the conversation to her husband. After all God gave the instructions to Adam before Eve was made. A dominant woman will emasculate a silent man, and a weak man will force a strong woman to take over. It is when you understand and walk in your perspective roles, you will perfect your purpose. Three things happened under Adam's watch... Adam did not protect the garden, he disobeyed the clear instructions from God regarding the Tree of Life and he did not protect his wife from the craftiness of the intruder. In fact, it is important to consider the verses following Eve's conversation with the serpent as recorded in the book of Genesis:

> *"When the woman saw that the fruit of the tree was good for food and pleasing to the eye, and also desirable for gaining wisdom, she took some and ate it. She also gave some to her husband, WHO WAS WITH HER, and he ate it."* Genesis 3:6 (NIV)

Throughout this episode, Adam was present but does not say or do absolutely anything to change the situation. He was passive when the serpent was spotted in the garden. He was passive when the enemy twisted the instruction and sifted his wife like wheat. After they sinned by eating of the tree, God sought out Adam because he was in charge and failed to protect everything he was given stewardship over. A lack of courage set the fall of a leader in motion.

Adam had compromised his relationship with his wife, but more importantly, he had compromised his

A Love Relationship by Design

relationship with God. A Pastor I know, once mentioned that this first woman was a masterful creation, possibly of perfected beauty. This is true, but no one should allow their desire for people to compromise their relationship with God. Furthermore, sin was not imparted until Adam's participation.

>Romans 5:12 (NKJV) says, *"...by one man sin entered into the world."*

The man is held accountable for what has been entrusted into his hands. In this case, this includes his woman (helpmate) as well as the other responsibilities that were given to him. The fact is, God wants the man to be a great leader as well as a great lover, but in order for that to be fulfilled, that man must possess character. One way to identify if a man is of Godly character is by observing the expressiveness of his wife face. The glory of it will be visible upon her.

Essentially, a man must be the pastor and leader of his home. He is not only responsible for ministering the Word of God but also accountable for ministering love and affection to his wife. To neglect her is to neglect Him, for they are one.

The problem today, is some men have been blessed with the woman God has given, but these men have no character, so they are unaware of what is in their grasp. Consequently, misusing and abusing the sanctity of the gift they've been blessed with. This will be discussed in detail in the chapter on **Perception.**

On the other hand, a woman can have a great leader and rebel against his leadership. Being that a woman acts and responds in multiplication, her actions, out of terms, can be detrimental to his confidence. This means she emasculates him, because of the need to get the last word. This could be a result of left over baggage from a previous relationship. This is why closure to past relationships are important before embarking upon new one. This is true for the male and female. Further, man may not recognize his wife's ability to compliment him for the same reason. Sometimes, God allows her to be removed for a time, so that He can prune the man, in order for him to grow into that awareness. Ultimately, man is responsible for the woman God has entrusted in his care.

When man's character is aligned with God's purpose the woman's reason is realized. When a man truly knows who he is, then he can better understand how to treat his queen. Furthermore, he knows why he was gifted with his unique and *characteristically different* helpmate.

When the balance of character God requires of a couple is present, no other woman can replace her. When we, as men, are with the helpmate God has created for us, the depth of her mind, the definition of her body, and content of her soul are uniquely created just for us, individually. All that she possesses was pre-defined for our destiny. This is the perfect expression of God's love for man.

Adam never challenged his wife's decision. This brings into focus the fact that most men are aware of what they are accountable for, but fail to maintain their position. Let's be transparent, sometimes to prevent denial from a spouse you bend some of your standards for temporary pleasure. Compromise is necessary as long as it does not interfere with God's plan and purpose. Adam was clear regarding God's instructions for him as the head of his household, but the simple act of communicating his understanding with his wife Eve was not present. His inability to speak up caused their fall in the Garden of Eden. Most importantly for men to note is that Adam was given clear instructions, but instead of leading he followed. Thus Adam's disobedience began when he failed to be the leader God created him to be. Some may disagree whether Adam was in the same proximity of Eve when the serpent tempted her, but one thing that we can all agree is that Adam willingly participated in an act that was against God's instruction.

In this case, being a leader is not defined as a dominator or controller. A true leader understands his

A Love Relationship by Design

position, as well as that of those around him. The President leads the country, but he is not an expert on everything. This is why he has a Cabinet made up of experts in different areas. They are the specialists who advise him on the particulars in the areas of their expertise. This helps the President make prudent choices in areas where he is not conversant.

From time to time, I am sure that even a powerful leader like our President is offered advice from his wife. If a man listens to what God has inspired in her, and heeds her advice, it will prove that a good woman can make a man even better. She can contribute an aspect to him that no other woman can, and he is wise to recognize that.

Sometimes, man misses the calling when he tries to control his wife. All he really needs to do is to recognize her strengths. She was made to compliment him; not to compete with him. She is not merely an assistant but a partner with him for the purpose of God and each other. She is not a threat but a contribution. If the woman is more economically wise than the man, then the man is still fortified, because he has a valuable member on his team who successfully fulfills that role and responsibility. In this case, his understanding of this strength should convince him to allow her to manage the finances, because she will do a better job. This does not mean that the man should turn his back to the families' finances, but instead allow the woman to take the lead role. This fills the gap, and that makes them one.

What makes a good leader is not man's ability to do everything but to recognize, utilize, and manage those strengths that surround him from within his wife.

A Love Relationship by Design

How We Fit

The dynamic design of male and female, as God created them, is a natural fit in every essence, spiritually, sexually, and socially. How we respond to each other in our actions will determine how well we fit together. When we think about fit, we consider how we are compatible. When we hear the word compatibility, we think of someone who is similar to us. But "compatible" means to exist in harmony with another. In relationships, men and women are different but God's intent is for us to live in harmony with each other. At times, it is not our similarities that make us compatible but it is our differences. One talks and the other listens and vice versa. One leads and the other follows. Sometimes it takes a extraordinary woman to balance an complex man. Eve was created as a help mate to Adam, which was to compliment him in his purpose in the Garden while adding companionship. It is when we complement each other that we are then truly made compatible, which does not always translate into seeing things exactly the same. A plug and an outlet are very different and useless on their own. But when they connect it becomes electrifying, as do men and women when they are synchronized.

A Love Relationship by Design

Galatians 6:7 (NKJV) *"Be not deceived; God is not mocked: for whatsoever a man soweth, that shall he also reap."*

When reflecting on the word sowing, we think in terms of agriculture. In order to get a crop, a seed must first be planted. This principle is also true in relationships. Women by nature are reciprocators, so in terms, the man will most likely reap what he gives her. When he sows love, most often he will receive love in return. On the contrary, if he cheats or abuses her, he may reap scorn and hatred.

In addition to man's responsibility, the woman must be conscious of the important requirements of her husband. When you hear the word compliment it is synonymous with respect. A man can feel belittled when not receiving the respect he desires from the woman. He can, in some instances, become so irritated to the point of losing all rationale. When you treat a man like a child, in terms of others, he appears to be forced to act like one. The one thing that constitutes the demise of a relationship is the lost of respect for each other.

In the evolutionary process of a developing relationship, it is difficult to see the outcome. In the beginning of a relationship, we sometimes only see the good characteristics or the best of the other person… this is the euphoria stage. Although, everything is great

A Love Relationship by Design

and well, reality will soon set in. Some call it the *potential* but I call it the *cleverness* of God. Much like when you first get saved, you are excited and it seems like God is moving promptly on your behalf. He is carrying you, and then suddenly you realize that now He requires you to walk by faith. At times, this can make it appear that God is absent when He is not; He just requires your faith to go to work. Once you have experienced this transition from newness in your walk to acting in faith, you are now even more motivated to get to the place, whereby what can be seen with your eyes and understood in the spirit becomes a sustainable reality. In this same way, relationships require work after the newness wears off. Challenges are a certain reality as the relationship grows toward the next stage.

When you have a spouse, how you treat him or her publicly is as important as how you do in private. For all general purposes, we sometimes don't consider what position we put the other person in with our actions. For the man, being a protector not only entails the physical, but also her mind, soul and emotions. Things that you might consider as insignificant can end up disastrous in the long term. Some public mistakes can damage your spouse's feelings in a way that may be irrevocable. Words and actions sometimes leave scars and embarrassment for life.

A Love Relationship by Design

Hebrews 13:4a (NKJV) *"Marriage is honorable among all."*

When you honor each other, you protect your partner from situations that can humiliate and demean them. For the man, your wife is the most important woman. I know you love your mom, but your wife is your first priority. Likewise, daddy's baby girl must hold her husband as the most important male in her life. Taking sides against your spouse says that they are secondary. Learn to discuss your matters in a private setting and do not publicly embarrass one another. The Bible tells us that, "For this cause man shall leave his mother and father and **cleave** to his wife..." This word "cleave" means to "attach" or in the Hebrew the word means "to glue, adhere or stick together." Simply, have each other's back.

It is important to honor your spouse in the presence of others. When a woman feels her spouse is more attentive to another woman, or when his behavior does not favor her in the midst of other women, then her integrity will be scrutinized by others, and will lead to a loss of security in the marriage. A good example of this can be as simple as a nice gesture, like giving another woman a ride to church without your wife, especially if she views the other woman as suspect.

A Love Relationship by Design

Cardinal rule, never allow yourself to be alone in a one-on-one situation with a woman of suspect, or one that can be a potential threat to your marriage. Even if nothing is going on, rumors and speculation can lead to doubts, suspicions and finally the dissolution of your marriage. The fact that we are human is enough to reconsider how we handle certain situations. This is where wisdom comes into play. Even if the other person is not suspect, always weigh the other alternatives to see what the risk factors are, based on your possible decision. The decisions must be mutually confirmed to prevent any future complications. If you feel the need to hide something from the person you love, then it probably not the wise thing to do.

In the same manner, a man wants to be certain that his woman is *his* woman. When she ventures beyond a certain point, he also becomes suspicious of certain behavior patterns. A man wants to feel needed and she is more dependent on someone else, he can become offended. In a sense, he feels useless. I know that we have friends for life, who are our gender opposites, but our spouse comes first and our friends must respect your marriage. Love each other enough not to land into compromising positions.

If you find yourself in a compromised situation, real or implied, be challenged to take the necessary steps to alter your stance. Coming to a consciousness of where

A Love Relationship by Design

you are, can be the initiator of a relational transformation. You should be open, adult, and wise enough to be honest with each other. Social media should be evaluated, because it has culminated into destructive force to the institution of marriage. It has used to both reconnect to past relationships and connect to new ones. The excuse has been I don't feel in love anymore or the relationship has ran its course.

Christianity is not based on feelings but on faith. This is also true with relationships and companionship. If your relationship is based on feelings, those conditions can—and will change, and may become an excuse for why it isn't working. The comparison between the candy bars, Mounds™ and Almond Joy™ is illustrated in a slogan that says, "Sometimes I feel like a nut and sometimes I don't." This simple statement typifies human character. Feelings can sometimes be deceptive. They can be the same component that brings you together or the antagonist that tears you apart. At times you must examine your feelings, so you could have the cognitive ability to reason logically within yourself before making detrimental decisions that can affect another person. Communicating with compassion can shield you from those negative forces; don't let your feelings ruin your partnership with each other.

Sometimes we conceive thoughts that give birth to feelings that are not conducive to reality. In other

A Love Relationship by Design

words, we create a false reality that affects our mood and perception. Mere thoughts that are not founded in truth can become believable, leading to anger over something that is just a figment of your imagination. When you act on them, it can cause a ripple effect that everyone is affected by. The objective is to work and overcome life's circumstances, even if you don't feel like it. Relationships are not perfect, and at times we may not feel like being in the company of one another. I am not encouraging you to accept bad treatment and behavior or to remain in unhappiness. But I am saying that there will be temporal moments of both major and minor incidents, which are completely fixable if you don't allow your emotions and feelings to dictate your actions. Intimacy is like this, God know our good and our bad, but yet he says I desire a closer relationship with you. That same process applies to our human relationships. Instead of drawing apart, use it as a mechanism to draw closer like a paradigm shift. We go to work not because we feel like it, but because we have a need or desire. When this idea is adapted to how you view each other, your relationship is not marginalized to mere feelings, but elevated to commitment. We desire the best out of others, but are we willing to render the same in return?

Women hope to find a leader and men hope to find a helpmate. Not just anyone, but one who can stand up to the original design. In the original design, man

A Love Relationship by Design

was given a purpose and then given a woman to help fulfill that purpose. Man was also given instructions by God about how to conduct himself in the garden. And today, we are given the Word of God as our instructions for living. Like us, both Adam and Eve missed the mark. Since the beginning of time, we have been a (WIP) work in progress. We are not perfect, but we should grow in perfection with each other.

Sometimes we jokingly comment that the other gender is slightly dysfunctional. The truth is we are inherently different and neither is dysfunctional in the nature of our original creation. Our roles are distinctly different and when we fail to understand that, we misunderstand each other. When we fail to occupy our roles that when we become dysfunctional.

Obviously, we all wish there was a gender handbook with all the rules, protocols and objectives that we could reference when situations call for it. Often times, we find ourselves feeling exposed and naked with no reference guide. In those dire situations, ignorance is not an excuse. Fortunately, there are biblical references that can better help us better understand and grow as one.

In this process, our thoughts must be transformed to think according to God's original intentions. We must revise our thoughts to level them against the truth of His

A Love Relationship by Design

Word. Often when we view the perfect man and woman in the scope of life, we become disappointed because we feel it is not realistic. It is only realistic when both individuals make the decision to put forth the needed work to bring into fruition a life together that parallels God's plan. The truth is no one is perfect, so don't set yourself up for disappointment by expecting that of the other person.

A Love Relationship by Design

Revising the Thought Process

This book is about revising and renewing your relationship. A fail-proof method is to constantly seek to improve, learn, and grow. This allows us to evaluate where we are at in our relationships and then make changes accordingly. It is crazy to continue doing the same thing over and over while expecting things to just work themselves out. In Fact, I have heard that this is the definition of insanity.

When a person sets out to lose weight, they must first alter their diet and begin to exercise. Both of these are important, not just any particular one. In relationships, we need to change how we process information and how we deal with each other. Our choices are the means that will determine whether we are willing to make the sacrifices to alter the course of our relationships.

> Proverbs 16:25 (NKJV) *"There is a way that seems right to a man, but its end is the way of death."*

This scriptural imperative is a caution or examination of the route for our lives, when everything seems to be going in the right direction, but is, in fact, on the path of destruction. This is a byproduct of our wrong thinking. For example, a man who was raised in

A Love Relationship by Design

a house where his mother took care of everything might believe that it is the woman's duty to handle everything. Growing up with his mother shaped the man's belief system. The man may never consider that his mother had no other choice because she never received help, because the father was absent..

  This is also true in marriages and relationships. Everything seems fine and good but definitive expectations can eventually lead to separation, envy, and even divorce court. Evaluating our relationships is often wise, as it allows us to review and revise our steps accordingly. What was good yesterday, relative to changing times, may be obsolete today. God does not change; however, seasons, people, and circumstances do. A good example of this could be made clear in a phone analogy. When I was young, cell phones had not made its mark on the world. We had one house phone to share with seven people, so we had to exhibit patience. It might be days before we had a chance to talk on the phone. In addition to this, if we were out, we had to wait until we returned home to make and receive calls. As technology changes, so do expectations. Just a few years ago, it was normal not to talk with a person for days, and it was not an issue. But today, if you don't respond to a text or call in a timely manner, you could end up receiving a text that states "This relationship is over". With everything at our disposal, we no longer have the patience we once had nor do we have the excuses we

A Love Relationship by Design

once had As a result, we respond based on cultural experiences. In certain cases, not adapting to the new norm could be a "deal breaker". A deal breaker is 'the catch' that a particular individual cannot overlook and ultimately outweighs any redeeming quality the individual may possess. As a result, the relationship has no ground to build a firm foundation. In some areas, this has nothing to do with any spiritual significance, just earthly circumstances we have grown accustomed to while others may have not.

The roadmap for our relationships must go back to our Creator as we relate to each other. Relationships are the heartbeat of society. When relationships are formed, communities are built. Communities are developed on a trust system, and when that trust is broken, the fiber that holds it together is weakened.

Just as communion was broken between man and God after Adam disobeyed and sinned in the garden, we all experienced brokenness in our human relationships today. Because of our imperfections, friendships, sibling, parental, and marriage relationships will all be tested. This is where returning to The Creator will make the difference. Although communion was broken, God gave us a link, Jesus Christ, through whom we receive God's spirit; that each day we may learn His purpose, and apply it to our lives and relationships; this is spiritual maturity. One of the most important tools

A Love Relationship by Design

learned through spiritual maturity is how to restore, and rebuild through constantly revising our perceptions and attitudes. This intuitive ability to recognize our flaws and initiate change is a process that will make us a new creation. A birthing process that starts internally.

This is what happened in my case. I asked God to teach me how to improve, and for Him to mold me to His standards in the area of man to woman love relationships. You see, there was a lot I did not know, but I was willing to learn. God dealt with me on three levels, which are Passion, Perception, and Purpose.

I was modified by the intrusion of sin
my identity compromised by Adam's fall.
But Jesus--His death at Calvary's cross
was designed to redeem us all.
Every day I am constantly changing.
Every day, again, I am made new.
Every day I am revised over and over
to someday, one day, look like you.
Because, God, you created me in your image.

Along with time, what we eat and drink changes our bodies. What we let settle in our thoughts changes our reasoning. What we allow to unnerve us modifies our emotions, and ultimately, how we conform to the image of Christ will modify how we will relate to one another.

> King David said, in Psalms 37:25a (NKJV) *"I have been young, but now I am old…"*

This passage indicates that life, the passage of time, brings about changes. This will limit us, in the dimming of our eye sight and the decreased mobility of our limbs, among other things. We have to adapt to these "life's changes", both uncomfortable and unwanted, but there are some characteristics that will improve with time. How we reflect on those changes will determine our response to them. By changing how we respond to others, we are effectively being a good steward over the relationships God has entrusted to us. We can improve those relationships by understanding and applying principles that result in positive outcomes such as learning to love each other unconditionally. The process of life is constantly geared to make us better than the day before. God loves us too much, to allow us to remain the same. The finished work on the cross proved this.

When it comes to men and woman there are virtually two different mindsets. Women are nurturers so their mindset is detailed, affectionate, and caring. Men are more physical thus, more direct and less sensitive.

A Love Relationship by Design

As boys, we were taught to be tough and not to cry, in order to make us strong. But, in some ways, those teachings desensitized us in how men relate to being sensitive to the needs of women. Battling these two differing characteristics can and will cause obstructions rather than solutions. Until we learn and accept why we were, intentionally, made different there will be an ongoing battle between the *one*. I say one, because God intended us to be one in marriage. It means to be unified and on one accord. Man was created in the image of God and then woman was taken out of man. The rib of man was removed symbolizing that man is missing something without the existence of his woman. He is complete but not whole. He is a man and functions as a man, thus he is complete; however, he is fragmented without her, because she holds a part of him. The complete man is whole only when the man and woman are unified with each other. Remember, God create her to compliment and correspond with man. Although, she is made from him, she is physically and emotionally different. In Genesis 2:23 "And Adam said: "This *is* now bone of my bones And flesh of my flesh; She shall be called Woman, Because she was taken out of Man.""

 Without each other, limitations exist in certain capacities. When you consider the fullness of God in humanity, it must have both the man and woman present.

A Love Relationship by Design

Because sin caused the original man to lose his identity, our wandering away from God's intentions broke the communion of man and woman, thus inhibiting a clear, God ordained, identity between the two. These are human defects and behaviors not designed by God. He gave woman to man, to complement and correspond with him. The skills he did not possess, she did. This is where the wholeness becomes pertinent. Sometimes we can take for granted that special person that God placed in our lives. Therefore, at every given opportunity, we need to consider how we view the gift entrusted to us and the stewardship over it.

Once we understand the significance of this concept, one can begin to change their behavior. In order to do so, we must retool how we think. I call it revision. When the first cell phone was introduced to the public sector, it was bulky, cumbersome, and expensive. Since then, technology has made them smaller, convenient, less expensive, and with an extensive variety of features. Unlike the cell phone that was made better, man has digressed from God's original design, we need to revise back to how we were originally created before sin tainted our identity. Revisions are intended to improve effectiveness and efficiency, or to correct defects.

In our humanity, we are full of defects and inefficiencies in how we relate, man to woman or

A Love Relationship by Design

woman to man. Unless we recognize and accept our flaws, we cannot even begin to change them. Everything is relative to something else. Winston Churchill once said, "Those that fail to learn from history are doomed to repeat it." The first step to change is to re-evaluate ourselves and then consider that how we think, as an individual, is not always right. No matter how brilliant we believe to be, how we think may be the downfall to our relationships.

> Romans 12:2 (NKJV) *"And do not be conformed to this world, but be transformed by the renewing of your mind, that you may prove what is that good and acceptable and perfect will of God."*

The obvious step is to think like God, since we were made in His image. This is done through being observant and applying His word to every area of our lives. Observation is what we see, but application is how we live it.

> Matthew 7:12 (NKJV*) "Therefore, whatever you want men to do to you, do also to them, for this is the Law and the Prophets."*

God loves us even when we do not love ourselves. He loves us in spite of ourselves. This culminates through the sacrifice of His Son, Jesus. We should love our significant others in such a way that it

A Love Relationship by Design

causes them to love themselves, in spite of them feeling unworthy of our love. Someone must initiate the action, in order for it to be reciprocated. When we treat love like a seed, it can sprout and grow yielding a return. This goes both ways because our humanity reminds us that we are fallible. In those moments, we find ourselves isolated from the very people God intended to love us through trials. There is a time for everything. This includes the good times and bad. It also includes the season or duration in which it lasts. Having someone to share those moments, is God's deepest desire for us. God is in eternity and we are set in time, so we must help each other adapt and transition through life's timetable. Having someone to inspire you on one hand, and then uplift and encourage on the other, is indispensable. It is God's way of showing His love through the one He gave the servitude to love you.

Time has a way of altering how you view life. The severity and duration of your experiences can distort how you see each other. This is covered through our imperfections. This is where forgiveness takes precedence over everything else.

Consider this, being put in a position of forgiveness only proves that God has given you the ability to show mercy. Due to our imperfections, eventually we will infallibly cause pain to our partner without planning or intention. Our human nature is full

A Love Relationship by Design

of emotions and moods; they are our life's highs and lows. They can sometimes cause tremblers that in turn cause turbulence and friction between you and the person you love. The external pressures of life can cause a carryover of tension that flows into and poses a threat to your relationship. Your connection to each other, or the idea of it, has an impact upon each of your feelings.. The right thing to do is to ask God to teach you to forgive when you do not have that intention, because, at some point, you will require the same in terms of forgiveness. Being able to forgive is essential to our growth. Learning to give and receive forgiveness is essential to the healing process. You never live free until you learn that forgiveness is not just for others, but it is for you.

The depth of God's love is so great that no matter how much we grow and learn of Him, we will never perfect his love. The idea is to strive toward God's love and offer mercy and forgiveness in the process. In Isaiah 43:25 *"I, even I, am He who blots out your transgressions for My own sake; And I will not remember your sins."* Can we, in fact, forgive like God? Not when we are boxed into to our human understanding of forgiveness. Most say, "I will forgive but not forget." I understand why we do, to prevent from being hurt again. What if God thought like we did? He said, "I will not remember them when speaking of our transgressions". This means you have been pardoned of

A Love Relationship by Design

those sins and they will never again be brought in judgment against you. Wow, what if those you love made this a practice, releasing you from your transgressions, never to be brought up again. How often do remind the other person, over and over, that they messed up. You will never heal under those pretences. I am sure that you could love on a much higher level with freedom, if you let some things go. Holding on to feelings of being mistreated by someone are the means that keep you in bondage. Holding on to those memories only give them power, making you forever captive to those individuals. When you let go, it frees you to love unconditionally, otherwise, you will never be open to love the way God intended. While you are stressing out about what happened, they are resting. Let it go and allow God to give you total victory. Pray for God to grant you wisdom and the guidance of the Holy Spirit in accomplishing this task. If we are to imitate Christ in His love, we should also imitate Him through His mercy and forgiveness. You will never heal and move forward by embracing the past.

God teach me to forgive.
Teach me how to forgive.
like forgiveness was intended to forgive,
forgiveness so intensely profound and deep.
There is a blood trace that links Jesus

A Love Relationship by Design

to a rugged cross at Calvary's hill.
Whereby hurt is healed, brokenness is sealed
and emptiness is finally filled.
Forgiveness is like a mega-structure.
over time, with character, forgiveness builds.
When you learn to forgive
you actually learn to live.
It is not something you earn,
as much as it is something you learn to give.
No limitations, no reservations, no restrictions.
Just hand it over to God, and let Him give the benediction;
non-preemptively, but redemptive, and non-discriminately.
It releases you and others from consented captivity,
like God unconditionally pours out His grace.
That proves and confirms His ability to love.
This forgiveness that God granted and planted
is sufficient for the entire human race.
For those who accept its unparalleled benefits;
past, present, and future sins can be erased.
A forgiveness, as far as I can tell...

A Love Relationship by Design

*it was blood spilled by a cat-of-nine tails,
a soldier's spear and eight-inch nails.
This type of Agape love was openly expressed.
So do not hold un-forgiveness,
tightly embraced to your chest.
Nor, let it abide and make residence in your current address.
Because it will eat away at your soul like a cancer
and consume with unnecessary stress.
You see, I am not forgiving others just to be forgiven.
Nor am I forgiving to be the better man.
I am a steward of God's Grace Manifesto,
a facilitator of forgiveness according to God's perfect plan.
If you could put your mind around this concept
and truly grasp the depth of what happened at Calvary,
you would willingly offer forgiveness yourself.
Then you too, could pour out forgiveness without measure.
You see, forgiveness gives, forgiveness lives,
and because of the exoneration of God's forgiveness ...
It forgives.*

A Love Relationship by Design

In the Beginning There Was Passion

There is a comparative thought that connects our thought process to the beginning of time. In the beginning, God created man perfect and without sin, until the enemy deceived Eve and then in turn Adam. We became defective due to sin and we are now being altered back to God's intended design through our Christian walk.

We were created in the "*Imago Dei,*" the image of God, but sin has tarnished our appearance. In the regeneration process, we are continuously being revised over and over. The word "passion" is from a Latin term, "*passio,*" defining Christ's suffering between Gethsemane and the cross at Calvary.

To have passion, there must be an igniter. Because we are God's creation, He made a sacrifice to restore our identity through Jesus' death on the cross. I can see a metaphor here in the relationship between a man and woman, because sacrifice is required for change to take place, even in our social relationships. What are you doing to restore what was originally your identity? Although, salvation can only be given by God, we are required to study God's word to transform our thought process. It takes effort and creativity to build continuity when nothing else exists to rekindle passion. Let us qualify this. Passion has much to do with intimacy, because intimacy means closeness. It means you are in touch with each other's thoughts, feels and emotions on levels that are spiritual, mental, and physical.

In the beginning, relationships can appear to be perfect. Unfortunately, there are subtle circumstances that nip away at the initial fire that you once shared. When a relationship begins, it is full of passion and vigor. You made time for each other and were considerate about the other's feeling. The short talks were meaningful, and even if what was said had no merit, the conversations with each other were more valuable than the content. Every moment together was quality time even if it were only minutes. Like spontaneous combustion, you would ignite anytime you were in each other's presence. Faces would light up, with playful intent and the joking over somewhat serious matters made them seem trivial. This eased you through rough spots. The mindset was totally different. To express your feelings, you bestowed gifts on the other person, even when you could not afford them. It did not matter, you found a way. When holding each other, you refused to let go only to hug and kiss several times more before finally building up the resolve to leave, when it was time. The passion was high and irresistible. Do you recall the moments trying to convince the other to hang up first because neither of you wanted get off the phone?

    When relationships get tough, the ability to rethink how you once felt and reacted can be the catalyst that initiates change. We often forget about the good times. Sometimes we look back and wonder what happened. Life's circumstances, jobs and even friends can wedge two people apart without them being consciously aware that they are growing apart in their thought processes. When you believe that you no longer have time for each other, you won't make any effort to make time. The truth of the matter is the success of a passionate relationship is dependent upon you. Passion is generated through meeting each other's needs consistently.

    We often fall prey to the notion that once marriage takes place that we have arrived and all the work is behind us. The truth is, all of the work has just begun, because now we have to sustain passion over time. We have to function in our normal day to day responsibilities, while also maintaining vibrancy with our spouse. This is work because even when fatigued, you have to labor through difficulties because of the needs of your spouse.

    Just as being revised back to God's original design, we must also revise our relationships back to the

A Love Relationship by Design

beginning, the exciting stage. Revisions need to take place when our spouse "representative" goes into seclusion. This is a familiar claim among those who are unhappy and considering leaving the relationship. A representative is the person you originally met who set the standards for a wonderful relationship. It is possible for that person to become complacent and believe it is un-necessary to keep doing all the little wonderful things they use to do. The worse thing that can ever be done is to take each other for granted. This can make the other person believe that their behavior was never genuine in the first place and that they were an imposter all along.

A man's natural response is to think the way he did during the pursuit stage of the relationship. In turn, the natural response for a woman is to respond the way she did while being pursued. All of the things that made you laugh and caused you to enjoy the initial flame of your first connection must be sought after and continued to be rekindled. These are the things that opened your heart to endless possibilities, were stimulating, and became passion igniters that must be continually pursed.

In the beginning of any relationship, we all put in overtime to make it work. In fact, we tend to go above and beyond our norm. It's like a jet airplane during take-off. It uses a lot of thrust to get off the ground, but once in flight the pilot moves the plane to cruise control. The problem is love relationships are different. Because a

A Love Relationship by Design

person's feeling are constantly changing, the human relationship needs constant validation, reassurance, and reaffirmation. There is no cruise control. Just going through the motions can easily be translated interest is fading. Relatively speaking, the effort it takes to get a relationship off to a great start may be substandard to that, which is required to sustain it. When we fail to do the necessary maintenance on our love life, we become a victim of failed statistics. Love has to be both maintained and sustained. Your love for each other must be interlaced with a deep abiding faith in God in order to be sustained while we maintain.

Love Defined:

I would say love is like a seed …a seed that is meant to reproduce and multiply because everyone needs love.
When that seed of love is spoken with life,
it converts to oxygen, and everyone in need of it suddenly begins to breathe love.
And when it is exhaled,
it mutates like an infectious airborne virus, unconditionally, reproducing and spreading deeds of love.
So cultivate and nurture love with all necessary action because your relationship will succeed on love.

A Love Relationship by Design

Love never fails.

A Love Relationship by Design

Understanding Affections

1 Corinthians 7:3 (NKJV) *"Let the husband render to his wife the affection due her, and likewise also the wife to her husband."*

When you read this passage in its entirety, it reveals an existential connection. Like an umbilical cord is the source of life to an unborn child, affection is a source and requirement for passion. The demonstration of affection produces an atmosphere that creates passion when done one to another in genuineness. In social psychology it is considered a form of reciprocity, according to Wikipedia. Reciprocity refers to the responding to a positive action with another positive action... a rewarding kind of action. Notice this action in the passage above starts with a seed sown by the man.. It is then interchanged by the woman in return. Not limited to just this area, but the woman's response is the direct result of the man's ability to cultivate.

I mentioned before that passion must have an igniter, and your act of giving sentiments of your feelings toward her will set her ablaze. This is the action of a wise man, and should be the rule rather than the exception. For this to happen we need to understand that there are many factors involved, some added and others

A Love Relationship by Design

removed, in order to create the igniter. Like a fire, oxygen, heat and fuel are needed. For passion to exist, affection, security, and desire is required. A person warrants these factors when they are not distracted, so distractions must be removed. Let us be transparent and dig a little deeper. If your mate is tired from a long day and still involved in chores or work, affections alone may not help. In this case, help your mate by eliminating some of their undone tasks like cooking, cleaning, homework, etc. This enables the other person to relax enough to receive and enjoy those affections.

A Love Relationship by Design

Physical Touch

Hebrews 4:13 (NAS) *"Marriage is honorable among all, and the marriage bed undefiled;"*

The scriptural essentials regarding sex are often referencing the external factors like fornication and adultery that can defile the marriage bed. In some marriages, couples act as if having sex is wrong, even talking about it can be taboo.

Physical touch is a form of affection. The literal understanding can be viewed as meeting each other's need in an intimate matter, through physical sensuality. When it comes to sex in the marriage bed, be confident that this is a gift from God given to share between husband and wife. It is honorable and held in high esteem. It is one of marriage's greatest benefits. Set the mood with an intimate bath followed with a passionate massage. Drop rose peddles on the floor for your Queen or King and set some mood music. Celebrate your marriage so you keep the outsiders, outside. Simply put, if intimacy is fulfilled at home, it will more than likely eliminate the desire for it elsewhere.

Physical touch is not just about passion but compassion. It is not only intimate but delicate. When someone is burdened, a simple hug provides healing. It provides comfort and security. When one hand touches another, it says 'we are connected.' When one holds another, it says 'relax because I have you.' This provides continuity and oneness. A woman receives and gives affection. She feels loved when embraced, massaged, and held. It is sense of being in tuned to every aspect of a person. If the man refuses to, or avoids touching her, she may feel rejected. She may not say it, but her emotions are a reflection of her identity.

In the middle of a passionate massage, go from hand to feet, running your hand through her fingers along with kissing gracefully and intimately. This is like a torch to dry grass. On the flipside, if a man attempts to embrace a woman and she rejects him, he may avoid attempting to touch her, because he has become confused by her disposition and attitude. He simply does not know how to read from her response the "why." He avoids holding her because he is unsure if his actions are right for the moment, so he simply avoids confrontation. This is why open and honest communication is important. Assuming can be detrimental to a relationship.

God created man to cultivate and to use his hands to bring forth a harvest. These same hands, if used correctly to caress, to be affectionate and to comfort his spouse, are an invaluable gift in any marriage relationship. If a woman believes that a man's touch is

A Love Relationship by Design

genuine, it will make her both receptive and responsive. Just the same, a man enjoys being touched, but maybe in a different fashion. When a man is touched by the woman in his life, it is to affirm his masculinity. Most men are stimulated by having their biceps touched or the occasional massage of their hair or head. It feeds his ego when he believes the woman is fascinated by his physical strength. Touching at the right moment is like playing keys on a piano because with every chord the melody creates passion and plays an intimate note.

A Love Relationship by Design

Passionate Intimacy

1 Corinthians 7:4-5 (NKJV) *"The wife does not have authority over her own body, but the husband does. And likewise the husband does not have authority over his own body, but the wife does. Do not deprive one another except with consent for a time that you may give yourselves to fasting and prayer; and come together again so that Satan does not tempt you because of your lack of self-control."*

I have to add a disclaimer here. Sometimes this text is taken completely out of context. I am speaking to a man's point of view because some often use this scripture as a bypass without putting in the effort to create passion that results in intimacy. When you rightfully demonstrate the things above, which in truth is the giving of each other, then everything else becomes second nature.

Intimacy can happen on demand for the man, but the woman's body by nature, doesn't work the same way. She has to be stimulated so that her mind and body can be in alignment with the physical act. The affection due should be consistent and continual, so that moments of intimacy would be the normal synergy rather than the exception.

A Love Relationship by Design

My kisses are in four movements,
like the orchestration of a symphony.
And, at times, improvisation and syncopation give
perfect pitch to sweet harmony.
A gentle kiss on the forehead
Introduces a melody to the scene.
This symbolizes being together forever,
but only God knows what that means.
I slowly caress one cheek,
and then the other with gentle affection.
The cambiata claps with streaming applause
for the resonance is perfection.
A kiss to the cheek says, "You look cute to me."
It identifies with the essence of your persona
and says, "you are as cute as can be."
The final movement is to the chin, slowly, gently
and all so delicately to the chin.
Kissing with a slow upright movement,
determined like a pilot making his final descent.
Lips so close ...so very close.
The chin tilts the jaw bone,

A Love Relationship by Design

which ultimately leads to this,
so take your time with this prelude,
it is the musical ensemble of the kiss.
I can kiss your back, neck and stomach,
for these places need no explanation.
This is a cacophony concerto
that is best left to the imagination.
There are more than a hundred ways to kiss,
depending on the moment of inspiration.
But your body will shout, "Bravo! Bravo!"
as a result of your passionate innovation.

Physical intimacy is one of the most passionate ways a man and his wife can express love for each other. Pastor Jeffery Johnson once said, "Making love does not start when you go to bed at night, but when you get up in the morning." It is the small, consistent, affectionate things that set the stage for a great sexual relationship. Sex was intended for procreation and the intimate, passionate expression of love between husband and wife. Any deviation from this transgresses against the will and purpose of God. I must be transparent , after my divorce, I did not know what to do with the sexual side of me. I suddenly began to realize how vulnerable I was. Can you imagine trying to say no to something you

A Love Relationship by Design

really desire? On occasions, I fell short, and the guilt was overwhelming. I asked for forgiveness only to find myself doing it again. Call me outdated, but I came to the conclusion, and reminded myself, that I needed a soul mate, not a flesh mate. I realized that if you are not disciplined, you can become immune to sinful intrigue, desires, and the act itself can become the norm.

Paul's letter to the church at Corinth sums it up this way in 1 Corinthians 10:13 (NKJV) *"No temptation has overtaken you except such as is common to man; but God is faithful, who will not allow you to be tempted beyond what you are able, but with the temptation will also make the way of escape, that you may be able to bear it."*

Actually, the writing of this book has also served as a means to keeping me busy and focused. I admit I love sex and realize that setting the scene for sex is not as difficult as I once thought. Our biological makeup warrants it, but our discipline controls it. Anytime there is a relationship between a male and female where attraction exist and it is close and affectionate, it causes them to want to express themselves in an intimate manner. This form of temptation is the hormonal appetite of sexual gratification. Sex outside of marriage ties your soul to that person. Some people are tied to multiple people, and while they are with one, they think of someone else intimately. It also ties you emotionally,

A Love Relationship by Design

but this effect occurs more for the woman than for the man. To the man, it is more physical and mechanical, but to the woman it is an emotional expression. This can become a stronghold if you are not careful.

When you have a relationship with God and possess any kind of moral obligation to Him, fornication or adultery will bear guilt. The Holy Spirit reminds you that you have stepped outside the will of God and that your body is His temple. In fact, you sin against your own body. In the moment, the act is pleasing, but once you are finished there is a sense of falling short. If a man has the desire for a woman and a woman for a man, this temptation will continue to be a nuisance and stronghold. Your escape route is marriage, but this does not mean you marry for sex. You must marry out of commitment and genuine love for each other, so consider building a strong friendship first before you build emotional ties. However, being married does not exclude you from unfaithful lustful thoughts. Practicing discipline while you are single prepares you for faithfulness when you are married. No one should let sex control them and limit their ability to make rational decisions.

Marriage cannot be sustained on sex alone because if it is extracted, there is no foundation on which the marriage can stand. Paul states that it is better to marry than to burn in passion. But, one must be

A Love Relationship by Design

careful to focus on making a connection with a soul mate, rather than a flesh mate. It is better to build on love rather than lust because love finds a way to navigate through the certain obstacles that will test the foundation of your relationship. The capacity of lust can tear down and breach the security and take root in one's spouse. When images of fantasy, pornography, and thoughts of external arousal exist, they promote the idea that your spouse is not enough. This can make them become distant and feel sexually undesirable. The fantasy distorts your reality and when the other person recognizes their position in an actual sense, it promotes insecurity. When contemplated fantasy thoughts are introduced to a partner, and they disagree, the other may be tempted to look outside for fulfillment of those desires. Be careful about the thoughts you conceive in your mind because they like a stick of dynamite that is capable of damaging everything within range.

In addition, the person with unfulfilled fantasy thoughts can become desensitized by the very habits they have created. This is true for both the male and female, especially when they prefer the touch of themselves over the touch of their spouse to stimulate arousal. There must be a mutual agreement on what both of you will enjoy. Each person must seek to satisfy the other over satisfying themselves, whereby in the end both are pleased. Creativity is good to keep the passion burning in your relationship, but be careful not to open

A Love Relationship by Design

doors that will compromise the integrity of your commitment to each other.

As a word of caution, opening one door can lead to opening a series of other doors, and this can expose your appetite to vain lusts. In the long run, this could lead to resentments and retaliations. Over time, small insignificant things compiled can contaminate the very essence of what God intended. But a genuine love for each other overcomes all obstacles.

Sexuality is beautiful when it is in its proper sequence. It is as close as you can get to a person. This expression harmonizes the beauty of a relationship. From my perspective, as a man, when God created woman, it was the most creative and masterful design of humanity. It was very methodical. Every curve and every bend was carefully thought out. When you are with that God-ordained person in marriage, it solidifies the basis of your relationship. The relationship should not be based on sex, but on genuine care, true love. If, for some medical reason sex was not an option, the relationship should still be sustainable. Love finds the way to adapt to a situation, even though it may be extremely difficult. This *"Eros"* or *erotic* love is meant to complement the relationship. It is not meant to be the foundation.

A Love Relationship by Design

There are many avenues for generating passion but the anonymity of true passion resonates from the unified, unselfish response to each other. The Song of Solomon's mysterious poetic beauty can't be expressed more intensely clear, than that of the Shulammite woman and the daughters of Jerusalem. It is apparently perceptible that something as simple as sensual kiss and verified love transcends even the coercion of an intoxicating drink.

> Song of Solomon 1:2 (KJV) *"...let him kiss me with the kisses of his mouth-For your Love is better than wine."*

Great sex stems from the spiritual, mental, and physical connections culminating into an off-the-chart expression of intimacy that can't be explained with natural words. Making love takes place far before any physical act of sex does. It is hinged on the woman feeling a sense of security. This is prime ground for sowing and reaping. Women are natural reciprocators. A man cannot expect to reap what he has not sown. On-demand works for cable, but not for a sound woman. Like everything in life, sex has a process.

A man who genuinely cares for a woman easily gives or sows into that woman. The woman takes what he sows and then multiplies that giving back even more. A woman always gives more than she receives. She is

A Love Relationship by Design

naturally built that way. A man gives her a seed, and she gives him back a child. When a man understands what makes a woman happy and deflects from her everything that makes her sad, that man is a protector and will have no problems receiving reward for allowing her to feel protected in his presence. Women require security and possess a desire for men to watch over them. When a man affirms his woman, it says, 'You are important. You are mine, and I am yours, and nothing will be allowed to come between us.' Telling her she is beautiful often and leaving notes on the dresser when leaving home reminding her of what she means to you, as well as confirming actions are all parts of the process that leads to great sex.

Included in the process to promote a healthy sexual relationship are those little things that you do throughout the day. Texting to say "I was thinking of you," will have her smiling among her peers, and will certainly get you rewarded in due time. Most men are satisfied with being respected the majority of the time. It is gifts of expressive love, not gifts of makeup and repentance, will make her feel loved, excited and compelled to reciprocate those actions toward him. Women express love differently, so a man must be careful how he loves her. Do not mistake cuddling for the opportunity for sex because sometimes she just needs to be held and understood,.

A Love Relationship by Design

Although males are more physical, believe it or not, they too have a sensitive side and will veer away from sex if things in the relationship are not right. Both men and women have mood swings, so be careful not tear down the relationship you are attempting to build up by dismissing these moods and categorizing them as personal problems of the other. We all possess feelings of both love and pain.

A Love Relationship by Design

Compliments, Notes and Coupons

Ephesians 4:29 (NKJV) *"Let no corrupt word proceed out of your mouth, but what is good for necessary edification, that it may impart grace to the hearers."*

Baby, your smile is equivalent to an enormous sunray.
Your brilliance pierces the clouds of a gloomy day.
Even when the clouds hang over our home,
for they may...
Your persona has the tendency to force them away.
Because You Are Sunshine!

Uplifting, unsuspected simple complements, words of affirmation, or encouragement, especially written on notes can go a long way. Because I am poetic and I have lived it, I know how simple words can make another smile or laugh could be the difference between a good or bad day.

Compliments are important. Notes and coupons are good options. I have a good friend who is notorious for this. He would send the women in his life "free

A Love Relationship by Design

hugs" daily via email just to make their day, and it worked. When compliments are a part of your everyday sentiments, she begins to realize this affection is not made just to get something in the moment. Your intentions are genuine, and the consistency validates your intentions. Remember, it is easy to sit in a barber or beauty shop and compliment people who do not play a significant part in your life, and then neglect the ones who we live with daily and love the most.

    These small memoirs practiced in a relationship have a spontaneous way of stimulating passion with minimal sacrifice. This concept generally has the least amount of words and effort, but is most effective, efficient, and one of the least expensive ways to spark romance in your marriage and make your feeling known. It also frees a spouse to make moves without questioning if the timing is right. Each person creates coupons based on the other desires, wants, and needs. I need to pause right here to qualify this, it is not about your wants but those of your partner. Understanding and fulfilling your spouse's love language is very important. With your partners desires in mind, you can then create a variety of coupons for hugs, kisses, massages, a night out for dancing, quality time, or intimacy. This gives the other person the opportunity to both redeem and offer services. The women may receive completed chores from their handymen while the men's signature dish is made. I know, in some cases, men are the cooks, and the women are pretty handy. Think of it as "Creativity over Capital." This section is a free spark of passion.

Mix things up making them a little more interesting by handing out a coupon for something you don't normally do. This shows effort on the part of the service provider. On a more serious note, it could be a prayer coupon, or even some time alone. Leave a note when departing for work like "I hate to go to work today because that means I will be apart from you," or making bold statements like, "You are a masterful creation-- every curve and bend, and when I get home later, I intend on taking a test drive." Believe it or not, simple little notes like this breathe new excitement and anticipation. Small disagreements and misunderstandings can be a catalyst that divides relationships, and in the same way, small appreciations can be the glue that keeps them together. Vacations and going out on dates are not always an option, but you should at least plan ahead and strive, within reason, to spend quality time together. Set aside one day a week to dedicate to each other. It is not always easy when you have kids, but from time to time find a baby sitter, so you can spend time for each other. This is a good way to break the monotony, but be resourceful when doing so. You are drawn closer through these small gestures and become more passionate. While men are visual, women are engaged by what they hear, so words are useful when used appropriately. Today, we are actually inspired and become active by applying God's written word to our lives, so it is important to write ideas down. These thoughts are then saved and later serve as a reminder. You can read the note as often as desired and those special moments relived over and over again.

A Love Relationship by Design

A Word in Season

P roverbs 25:11 (NAS) *"Like apples of gold in settings of silver Is a word spoken in right circumstances."*

We have often heard "Sticks and stones may break my bones but words will never hurt me" but the reality is, words do hurt. When someone you care about says harmful words, it can leave a lasting impairment that in some instances can have an everlasting effect. On the other hand, hearing the right word, at the right time, from the right person can have a life changing effect. This is especially true in marriage. When a woman needs to be affirmed or a man needs to feel appreciated, it must come at the right time and from the right person. If a co-worker praises a woman telling her that she is beautiful or is of great value, it will not carry the same weight or meaning as when her husband tells her the exact same words.

The co-worker's words may be flattering to the woman but may stir an issue with her husband, because he is one who should be saying it. She may like hearing it but she will want to know why her husband isn't saying it. It frustrates her that others around her recognize the obvious, yet her husband never tells her. This generally spurs feelings of being taken for granted

A Love Relationship by Design

and resentment. This is especially true when the man affirms her of his love after she confronts him. A woman wants to hear it from her man without prompting. For the male ego, there is the desire to be a good provider and a yearning for acknowledgement when he is. In a sense, the man seeks security in his own way. He requires confirmation and if the woman does not provide him with it, the man can begin to question his manhood, feelings of inadequacy may rise or he may begin to feel under appreciated. When his wife confirms the appreciation of his provision, the man feels a sense of accomplishment and that his labors were not in vain.

The needs for men and women are different in most cases. Women requirements are to feel wanted while men requirements are to feel needed. When a woman is not affirmed she feels empty and that can translate into problems that when left unattended can lead to divorce. Likewise, a man who feels unneeded may lead him to search for companionship that allows him to operate in his natural position as a man. This can conclude with - an extra marital affair. It is not always about what you hear, but from whom you hear it. When the right words are spoken and heard with correct timing, those words can ultimately be the resurrection of your marriage. Never leave anything concerning your feelings about your lover up to question. Kind words of appreciation and support are especially needed in a marriage when couples are facing obstacles. Be mindful

A Love Relationship by Design

of your spouse's needs and reassure them that you are standing by their side with support and encouragement. It all comes down to recognizing what is of value to you. That should be your spouse.

A Love Relationship by Design

Bearing Each Other's Burden

Galatians 6:2 (NKJV) *"Bear one another's burdens, and so fulfill the law of Christ."*

Relationships are often strengthened only after they are tested and tried. There is no better feeling than knowing that the one you love is there with support and love. In the wedding vows, the minister often says, "in sickness and in health, for richer or poorer," which means on both sides--in the good and the bad times of life--you will be tried. When a person stands with you in the most difficult of times, you have a true mate. Even though there may be times that they feel like giving up, a true mate will, with certainty, press through the darkest hours and stand with you. Bearing burdens suggests that you obtain help carrying those hardships that can weigh you down. Burdens are easier to bear when someone is willing to help you carry them. I have a friend who had to permanently bring his mom into his home because she was sick. This would have been a burden for many, but instead his wife stepped in and took care of his mom as if her own. This took the burden off my friend, in fact, his wife's actions helped him carry the burden. His comment was, "Ooh, wee, man! God blessed me with a wonderful wife. I could not have done it without her."

A Love Relationship by Design

The very fabric of his relationship with his wife is strong and continues to grow stronger.

When you experience hardships and bear each other's burdens together, it makes it most difficult for others to come in divide that strong bond . Knowing you possess a rock solid relationship with someone who has your back, you dare not risk losing it for something unproven. Life's tests results in relationships growing roots that run deep. Helping carry burdens draws partners closer which in turn helps passion between two individuals grow.

Even everyday encumbrances can affect intimacy in a marriage, especially when the woman is carrying the full load of responsibility; cooking; cleaning; helping the kids with homework; laundry; managing household expenditures. Understandably, the woman will be exhausted at the end of the day. It is not just physical exhaustion but mental exhaustion as well. Just thinking about all that she has to keep up with will cause her stress. When a woman feels stressed, she is least likely to desire sexual contact. This is even more so when she works outside of the home. As her husband relieving her of at one or more of those burdens and responsibilities, gives her a chance to relax. In the same manner, understanding a man's point of view for relieving stress, which is being sexual, can aide both

A Love Relationship by Design

parties in reaching a compromise to spread the load and to meet in the middle, effectively helping one another.

Love does conquer all and allowing the Holy Spirit to teach you how to love one another will help you realizes this truth. No obstacle or barrier set before you will stop your forward movement. The vision becomes unified, and everything becomes, a proclamation of "let's do this together... let's get through this together... let's accomplish this together." You then become more passionate about each other, which will weed out the possibility of infidelity and strife in your relationship. That's when we discover the truth in the wedding vows that states, "What God has joined together, let no man separate."

Love finds a way...
True Love finds a way to weather life storms.
Trials will come for a season, but so will the calm.
But you have a greater chance to survive
when you are embraced in each other's arms.
Love finds a way to teach you
that everyone you date is not your soul mate.
Every season is not your season.
So seek God first, and patiently wait.

A Love Relationship by Design

Everyone who you hang with is not your friend.
Everything that feels right is not right.
Some even equate to sin
when the fortitude of physical love is applied.
It cannot be denied.
In it you should abide.
So when you go through the fire of life,
your love becomes proven and tried.
Because strength comes in numbers
if agreement and continuity reside.
…there is no free ride.
But love does find a way, if it is love not lust,
Because lust you can't trust.
It disperses in the wind like particles of dust,
so here I must say…
Love, only love, finds a way.
When companies downsize,
your love stock should ultimately rise.
Because your dependence is on God,
you have each other's back and look toward the skies.
Love's truth is tested when trouble comes.
You are attuned to be your best.

A Love Relationship by Design

Because love finds a way…

It finds a way to heal from hurt.

It calibrates your life to be spiritually alert.

Yes, forgive, because we all need to be forgiven

in one way or another.

Forgiveness symbolizes love *Agape*-style

and *phileo* love, having true love for each other.

Love even finds a way to love its enemy,

which begins to be a sacrificial win for me

because it expresses my growth and maturity.

Ultimately… ultimately… ultimately,

love does find a way!

A Love Relationship by Design

Man's Passion for His Wife

"*Husbands, love your wives, even as Christ also loved the church, and gave himself for it*" Ephesians 5:25 (NKJV)

Did you get that? With the same passion that Christ loved us; men are to love their wives; with the same spirit; the same character; the same personality as Christ. This love encompasses long-suffering, protection, and perseverance. It is no small task. In fact, it's a sacrifice. The man's responsibility is to be priest, provider, and protector of his home. He is to be obedient to God, so he can reap submission from his wife, as she reaps submission in her children. Giving of you is not merely a suggestion but a requirement.

The word *submission* in the Greek is "*hupotasso,*" a military term meaning, "To rank under or to position under." Men, recognize the position or rank of your wife in the family. She is a helpmate with the responsibility of corresponding and complementing. She is a natural reciprocator. She multiplies life and gives it back in abundance. Women, recognize the rank or position of your husband. He is the "houseband." His position is to hold the family together under the order of God. When one recognize the respective roles as God

A Love Relationship by Design

intended them, your marriage will grow and passion ignites.

The Bible tells us in Mark 10:9 (NKJV) *"What therefore God hath joined together, let no man put asunder."*

Often times we question why relationships don't last. The first is that not every relationship that exist God joined. We make decision based on different reasons, and not all are the right reason. The other is God can place people together and we can be destroyers of God blessings to us. Like any relationship, if you do not nurture it, it will wither and die. Ask God to order your steps and recognize if you are suitable for each other. The key is to make sure God was in the process of your marital relationship.

Giving Sacrificially

Love is an action word; meaning that saying the word love is only valued when the act of love is involved. A primary example of this is God's love toward us.

> John 3:16 (KJV) *"For God so loved the world that He gave His only begotten Son, that whosoever believeth in Him shall not perish but have everlasting life."*

In today's economy, it is easy to feel we don't have the resources to give in the way that we desire. I submit to you, that true giving has nothing to do with money or material possessions but has everything to do with the sacrificial giving of yourself. In the beginning, God "*bara,*" which means, "He took nothing and made something." This is the creative nature of God. Since we resemble God, we are genetically coded to heighten our creative side when nothing else exists. When one puts forth creative effort that causes uniqueness to rise to the surface, it will promote health and hope for that relationship. It tells others that special thought was given into the situation. It then becomes priceless.

A Love Relationship by Design

Consider going to the hobby shop to purchase construction paper and then cutting out hearts or playing cards to simply enjoy each other's company. You will discover that the outcome is better when the actions are more personal. Your one-of-a-kind gift is better than the one duplicated thousands of times. It can be recognized as gift given with passion.

A Love Relationship by Design

Perception and How To Change It

We use philosophy, sociology, physiology, and theology to try and gauge God's methodology. But He is the Creator, and we are the creation. This cannot be fully comprehended with our psychology. We are limited in our capacity, and only see a portion of God's totality...That's our reality!

When a relationship begins between a man and woman, some perceptions are developed due to how we falsely present ourselves to the other, especially when we don't have a full understanding of the other person. We tend to be, by all means necessary trying to impress by being something or someone we are not. Further, this can cause attachment to the minor detail of a person. I call it "101 Attractions." When we are sold on the elementary characteristics, like mere physical attraction, we could be setting ourselves up for failure. The other person can look great outwardly while still being infested with ugly traits; come from a good home, but not always have good motives.

Attraction exists, and at times, we humans can easily become attracted to the wrong people. Our vast differences can cause a large sway in perception. We are naive at times, and create a view about a person that is fictitious. This is because we want the person we are

A Love Relationship by Design

with to be the ideal one, looking past the obvious warning signs and indicators. Everyone can see the truth, but us. It is important to be equally yoked with a like-minded person, one with a common faith and belief system. You must be patient to become friends. In this you can make rational decision. On this premise, one can build a solid foundation, even though there will still be some differences. This is because we are all unique and our personal experiences shape how we think. Attraction takes on many facets… physical, mental and spiritual attraction, are among some of the characteristics that cause one person to gravitate toward another. In most cases, it is either confidence that implies security, good communication or it is physical attraction that is the initiator. As you journey beyond the first few dates without incident, a mutual attraction that exceeds the physical, such as mental stimulation, and discovery of similar interests and values, begin to heighten the experience. It is like gravity.

Gravity has strong power, for in such it draws.
When you become subject to it, it has just cause.
It facilitates its own rules;
you are powerless to its force field.
It attracts inanimate objects
and regulates and stamps its own seal.
To be drawn toward someone is like gravity,

A Love Relationship by Design

for you succumb when you least expect it.
Attraction writes its own rules,
so your best bet is to just respect it.
I am attracted to your spirituality
for the certainty draws me near.
It paints a clear picture for me
that Christ roams in your atmosphere.
I am drawn toward your mind,
your creativity and intellect define...

    In the beginning of relationship bliss, you can sometimes become oblivious to unconsidered realities. Emotions begin to reign over reality and it can be compared to good and bad cholesterol. The connection can either lead to a healthy or an unhealthy relationship. For example; you notice emotional ties that begin to develop because you talk on the phone for hours. You think about each other all the time and can't stand being apart. Suddenly, one person is going at full speed while the other is slowly hitting the brakes, which causes an emotionally crash when the speeding person realizes they and the other person is not connected in the same manner.

A Love Relationship by Design

It is important to regulate your emotions and communication so that you are in step with the other person. Your spiritual and mental awareness have to keep your emotions in check. When starting a friendship, you must constantly make your position clear. If a person desires to just be friends, then there are certain lines that cannot be crossed; otherwise you will be sending mixed signals. The man must not fuel the woman's emotions by his affection, because it can be translated to mean 'more than just friends.' When friends act upon feelings of passion, even kissing, the relationship moves passed the point of "just being friends." Fundamentally, the Word makes it clear that physical relationships are reserved for the institution of marriage. You may think adding a physical dimension to your relationship won't affect your feelings, but time will prove otherwise. When a couple becomes sexually intimate, it says we are together and committed to each other. In fact, you become one with that person in that act.

Men, if you are intending to be the head of your home, then the task begins when you are dating. No matter what a woman is willing to offer, it is your responsibility, in God's eyes, to protect and direct her virtue. Leadership and Godliness begins on the first date and sets the course for your potential life together. Taking a woman's virtue without the sanction of marriage is against God's direction.

A Love Relationship by Design

Never allow your emotion or physical attraction to dictate your actions, especially in the beginning of your relationship, as you can very easily become a one night stand. Within the first six months, if you are losing yourself in a person you need to regroup and pace yourself. It is much too soon as you are still in the early stages of identifying each other. One thing can change the course and leave you emotionally broken. As you begin to write the chapters of your love together, be cognitive that marriage is the goal that will solidify the love that you have for each other. It is easy to become complacent; whereby you begin to enjoy the benefits of marriage without the commitment. God honors marriage because it is a commitment for life.

Do not allow your desire to have someone in your life blur your rational thoughts. This can allow someone to play on your emotions. Feelings are like a dust storm, causing you to not see clearly until the dust settles. The excitement about finding that right person can be extremely deflating upon realizing that they are not really who you thought they were. Especially when you created a pedestal, that made them appear to be larger than life. Embarrassment can cause you to spiral because you presented someone too highly before really getting to know them. You can find yourself asking more questions than there are answers.

A Love Relationship by Design

At the start of a relationship, you have to possess an open/closed mindset. One that is open enough to the possibilities but closed enough to move on, if the relationship does not work out. When you connect intimately, it becomes exponentially more difficult to detach from the relationship emotionally. When a relationship starts out wrong, it usually ends the same way; hence it must be driven by the right motives and intentions if marriage is the long term objective.

If you decide to move on from a relationship, make certain you close the doors behind you or those doors can re-open exposing the skeletons of your past.

Proverbs 18:22 (NKJV) *"He who finds a wife finds a good thing, and obtains favor from the LORD."*

The word *"favor"* is translated in Vine's Complete Expository Dictionary as meaning, "acceptance, goodwill, or approval." The Hebrew word for *"finds"* is the word *"Matsa"* which means, "to happen upon, to come upon, to encounter, and to fall in with." Men usually go on a recruiting mission trying to find the right woman, but what the scripture is saying is that we need to recognize her when she comes our way.

This is evident with Adam and Eve during the time of creation.

A Love Relationship by Design

Genesis 2:22 (NKJV) *"Then the rib which the LORD God had taken from man He made into a woman, and He brought her to the man."*

In other words, he encountered her and knew it. They both did. Adam recognized himself in her because she held his rib. She was a perfect fit, a custom tailored woman, not just for companionship but for purpose. This means you must understand your purpose in order to identify what fits. Just because a person is Christian, and loves God, does not necessarily mean that they are suitable for you. In Genesis, God made Eve specifically for Adam's purpose in the garden. What is applicable to us, because God is all knowing, is to understand the direction we are going and ask God for that person who is moving in the same direction.

Another thing to consider is children. Not only agreeing on having children but, if you already have children, is that person right for them? Your kids are the first responsibility and priority.

For the man, the reality is that not every woman is designed to go where he is going or capable of undertaking the mission he has been given. Only a woman crafted specifically for that particular man will last. The Word tells us that God orders a righteous man's steps, so you can rest assured that He knows what you need to fulfill the assignment. Let God bring her to you.

A Love Relationship by Design

Changing our Perception

How we view God, will ultimately determine how we view each other. If your thoughts are twisted in relation to God, then your thoughts will most likely be twisted in relation to the one you love. After all, we are created in His likeness.

> Proverbs 23:7a (NKJV) *"...for as he thinks in his heart, so is he."*

James Allen, an English author and poet once said, *"A man is literally what he thinks, his character being the complete sum of all his thoughts."* The truth is, the sum of all of your thoughts, at certain times, can be completely false or a mere perception of reality. Sometimes, we believe that calling out scripture obligates God to act on our behalf. It is not the words of scripture that moves God to act, but is the faith that you have in His Word that moves Him. A large portion of us would worship the gift instead of the gift Giver. Yet others are arrogant enough to believe that they are the only ones who have access to God. Some, self-proclaimed Christians, actually believe this and one of the biggest obstacles to our having the correct perception is our theological misunderstanding of God. We view God as some cosmic bellhop who can be

A Love Relationship by Design

instructed on what to do. God is our infinite Creator and deserves to be worshipped and adored by us finite beings. We are to magnify Him. That is, to see and respect Him for who He is, and not for what we want Him to be.

> Isaiah 55:8 (NKJV) *"For My thoughts are not your thoughts, nor are your ways my ways, says the LORD."*

This is also true in the relationship between a man and woman. Our thoughts can differ and sometimes our relationships are based on what we think and believe, rather than what we understand and know. Perception is not always the truth and quite often is just someone's version of it. Perceptions are often developed in the initial stage of dating and courtship and can serve as the adversary sometimes causing misunderstandings. We all perceive things differently. A good example of this is a teacher requesting a class of students to write a short paper on what they view from an abstract painting. Each individual sees the painting from their own perspective based on images and experiences relevant to themselves. A man and woman can receive the same email; while a man will read its content; a woman will read into it. She looks for more than just the words that are written. She sees in multiplication.

A Love Relationship by Design

As I look out the window of life I see,
only things that surround just me.
But in a another place, there is a woman
who sees things differently from her own view's span.
We perceive that we are beholding mysteries unknown
To gaze from the other…
yet every man and every woman,
Possesses their own perception.

A Love Relationship by Design

The Hunter

When you first meet a person there is no sure way of knowing if the relationship will last. You may know if they peak your interest but there are too many unknowns that have to be answered in order to determine longevity. A person should want to leave their signature when dating. A *signature* is something that uniquely identifies them; it is that lasting impression, and that makes the hunt for another interesting. Dating has changed due to time constraints and lack of patience. Today, time is of the essence, so as a result, many conform to efficiency dating.

A friend of mine once wisely stated: "Many conduct dating as a business." They search for qualified applicants and go through the interview process, sometimes multiple ones simultaneously, so they have something to compare against. They first engage in friendships with limitations, meaning they talk while leaving all the emotional discussion outside. Why? Because emotions can cause one to become bias in the 'hiring' process. One may like the applicant's personality, but do they meet the requirements on the business side? The best name for this stage is "friends with possibilities."

A Love Relationship by Design

Dating multiple people, at the same time, will always leave someone on the outside looking in. The thought that you can't expect everyone you meet to "be the one" dismisses the moral call to not hurt someone by reasoning that you must remain open minded. By thinking outside the box, you are not emotionally damaged in the process. You may like many of the candidates, but only one can fit the criteria perfectly. Only one can make the final cut, however you must be certain that the one you chose possess the potential qualities for a lasting relationship. This is no different than online dating. You go through chats and even a date or two with potential prospects before you narrow it down to the one that best suits you. Be careful that you are not naïve, and think that a person is exclusively chatting without you, because it is possible that they are evaluating who best suits them, in the same fashion as you are.

For the man, this typically places him in the role of the "hunter." From the woman's point of view, she is positioning herself to be "prey."

The modus operandi or M.O. of a hunter is based on character and personal requirements. He is attracted to a certain type of woman and uses certain tactics to attract what suits him. The types of hunter vary, and are often cross-functional in nature.

A Love Relationship by Design

An introvert man operates differently than an extrovert, and the more you analyze the two, the more the differences become clear. Some personality traits are parallel while others will intersect when it comes to the process of the actual pursuit. For this reason, I will summarize the different types based on the hunter's intent, on a man's embodiment. Here, both male and female must use discernment because not everyone is living a Christian lifestyle even if they claim to be. Watch their fruits.

The ***Recreational Hunter*** hunts for the fun of it and is really not serious about what he catches. He plays with it, shows it off for a while and then turns it lose back to from where he found his prey. He is only serious enough to hunt but not serious enough to keep what he catches. The process for him is the entertainment, showing that he has the capacity to pursue; yet he does not have the appetite to cook it. He teases and then backs out when the person of interest wants to get serious. Not the 'settling-down' type but is good to hang out with for fun without the fear of being pressured into a commitment. For the Recreational Hunter, this is just his way of being social and passing time.

The ***Irrational Hunter***. Whatever he catches he tends to eat. This person hunts everything; is careless and free spirited. He is like the Recreational Hunter

A Love Relationship by Design

except he cooks first, eats, and then tosses away the remains of his catch. However, like a scavenger the irrational hunter will return to the remains of what he has tossed if the opportunity affords. Everything appears delicious to him and upon spotting something better he chases that also. Anyone who chooses to lay with the irrational hunter will acquire fleas. He is not concerned with his own wellbeing or others and acts without thinking.

   The ***Aggressive Hunter;*** far more focused and does not waste time. He zeroes in on the catch, traps his prey and then is gone. He usually possesses an alluring confidence that catches the attention of his prey. His daring personality unravels with an adrenaline rush that tunes her into his frequency. His aggression is viewed as charming and she is turned on by his ability to take control. He seems fun and adventurous because she never knows what to expect from him, also perceived as leadership skills. Not to say he could not be a leader, but this can sometimes be misread when, in fact, is really not the case. The Aggressive Hunter, can convince his prey with verbal tenacity and wit, not requiring good looks, only eloquence of speech and the understanding of when to use it. Innately, the prey follows instantly as these outward characteristics portray the image of a man who knows what he wants. On the flip side, this could also be the guy she can't rid herself of if and when she realizes he is all smoke and mirrors.

A Love Relationship by Design

If she decides she wants out, his aggressive nature may make it difficult to escape without a struggle.

The ***Methodical Hunter*** is very clever as he baits and waits holding patience as a virtue. He puts enough of himself out there to spark an interest but not enough to truly reel the prey in. The methodical hunter is subtle in his schemes by doing small insignificant things that flatter and never bore. He behaves systematically different in comparison to the other hunters; easily cutting across the grain with his demeanor making the woman feel special, through clever mental games. The Methodical Hunter is a thinker and his mental conscripts plan out his capture over a period time. The woman he pursues remains mostly confused as she is never sure if he truly is interested in her or not, due to the great affections he displays and bestows, though never going in for the kill. She at times, will conform to his game playing with the hope that he will make her feel special. He, by far, is the most dangerous hunter because he is not shallow, and at no point can be figured out or boxed in by her. His patience makes him elusive. When he speaks her body reacts without him ever touching her. He uses reverse psychology dealing with her mind, which in turn triggers emotions. This behavior pattern, in the end, will convert her into the hunter. If the woman cares for the man, she may take the role of pursuer, as a result of him moving too slow. This man is the one the woman remembers as she fans herself. After being touched by him, she believes she has never been touched in this way before. The fact is; it is all in her mind. Her thoughts are irrelevant, because he has touched her mind, and her body thinks it was his hands. His anticipated touch has heightened her senses, but his intent is merely a figment of her imagination.

The most powerful hunters are the ***Purposeful*** and ***Influential Hunters.***

The ***Purposeful Hunter*** pursues only a certain type allowing most prey to pass by because they do not meet his specifications. He is picky and with the exception of looking for certain qualifications, is somewhat similar to the ***Methodical Hunter,***. Allow me to draw a parallel picture, from a business perspective. If operating a business, he's searching for an accountant. If a minister, he pursues a qualified First Lady to share his ministry with. The end purpose dictates the prey. The hunter's desires are clear and he will not rest until she is found. The purposeful hunter sees past mediocrity and has no desire for short-term, "in the moment" relationships. He is usually extremely cautious in his selection because the captured prey must keep him satisfied for a life time. His purpose for existence, her ability to further that purpose and the prey's ability to relate to him makes her attractive. Their mutual passion for purpose can spill over into their love life because passion is self-combustible when two lives are united.

Finally, there is the **Influential Hunter**. He generally uses his money and influence to sway the game. He's usually in search of a trophy or momentary entertainment. Gifted with the power of influence that others cannot afford, he introduces the prey to a life of elaborate living. Typically after sampling a taste of this lifestyle, her appetite will change. The danger in this situation is that the woman falls in love with his resources, rather than the man. This superficial love can pose trust issues on both sides. For her, there is the constant concern over his power to persuade another woman. For the Hunter, the knowledge of his vanity influence being presented by another in the same or greater fashion. The concept of love is perverted to a convenience that suddenly becomes inconvenient. Not all men who possess wealth use such power and influence to manipulate situations; usually only those who are not skillful or patient enough to explore deeper than what money can buy. The woman in this scenario is generally the one who discovers that love can't be bought; long after it is too late.

Like the male, women are attracted to qualities that fit their character, so based on this basic attraction; she is captured by one of the hunters. Usually, a woman is drawn toward the man who takes control because she

A Love Relationship by Design

is instinctively looking for a leader. Authority is attractive to most, but it not always the norm. Most attractions are learned and attributed to what we have experienced in our upbringing. Attractions are also inspired by what has been taught by your faith. Women are looking for a man like Boaz. By biblical account, we know he was an upstanding man in the community, a worker, owned and possessed land and had favor in the eyes of his woman. A woman wants to be secure in knowing that her husband favors her. A woman yearns for a 'Boaz,' or Boaz's little brother, and might even settle for a Boaz's cousin, as long as he possesses similar characteristics!

The woman, who is one with her husband, will make every effort to insure that her husband is successful in his purpose. Yet, we realize that due to prior experiences in life, some women do not respond like suitable helpers. Their past relationships, culture, and upbringing may have stripped them of their natural God given attributes. When a man is placed in a position where his spouse does not respond in a helpful manner, he must do what he was created to do—CULTIVATE! By sowing love, affection, and spiritual strength, the man can resurrect her innermost attributes that were suppressed by past wounds. When a man completes this task, he will have breathed new life back into her and she will become an extreme blessing. In this process, it is imperative not to simply look for information, but to search for ways to connect and build trust. The woman also wants a provider, and will respond with actions that give back and nurture what is given her.

A Love Relationship by Design

Provision

One of the biggest perceptions encountered centers around provision as it refers to economics and the man. At one point in history, it was expected that the man provide for his family making certain that the woman did not have to work outside her home. The Proverbs 31 woman may not have been the main artery for income in the home but was still a major contributor in her own way. What she did or did not make and sell was far outweighed by how adept she was at managing her household.

A provider is one who meets needs. Provision is defined as predicting a need before it happens and then meeting that need when it occurs. This requires the man to be a visionary and a planner. This also requires actions to carry out that plan. There is a famous saying that indicates " We don't plan to fail, we just fail to plan." Putting yourself in position for a serious relationship is important. The added frustrations of trying to balance a relationship and positioning yourself financially can be challenging. Often the definition of a provider is misunderstood. A provider seeks to meet needs and not necessarily wants.

A Love Relationship by Design

2 Thessalonians 3:10 (NKJV) *"...for even when we were with you, we commanded you this: If anyone will not work, neither shall he eat."*

What was meant by Paul's letter was that man must be adamant about taking care of his family. . The issue is not with those who could not work, but with those that would not work. Translated for today, if a man does not have the character, concern or care to provide for him, then what makes him capable, accountable and driven enough to provide for a family. The key is in the dating process to recognize his position of providing but on the flipside the woman's view on spending and help wisely managing resources. Some consider a man who cannot take care of certain material possessions to not a provider, but this is completely false. The qualifier is whether or not the possession is a need or want.

Today, it is common practice for women to work outside the home and manage businesses. Of course, this is either out of obligation or decision, -, but, in addition had a lot to do with women being forced to care for themselves. Because of this they have developed an economic independence from men. This is not necessarily a bad thing, unless the woman uses it in arbitration against the man as an argument to say I really don't need you. When either the man or woman uses their economic clout to disregard the other, it divides the

A Love Relationship by Design

home. Personally, I would love to be a provider, whereby working would be an option for my wife, but this opportunity is not always afforded to everyone.

Other issues facing couples today are the economy and men losing their ambition. Men dream big but reality is only a small percentage of them reach an optimum level and soar beyond mediocrity. Although the possibilities are endless, stewardship still requires discipline. You can have a great job making plenty of money and still struggle with providing for your family if spending is not controlled. In our current economy, two incomes are often required to sustain a secure economic situation. In the event only one spouse is working, it requires balancing the budget and cutting back on nonessentials to prevent over spending.

When the man is the sole provider for his household, it is incumbent upon the woman to help make sure a budget is followed. As a wise woman, her ability to stretch available funds is one of her greatest accomplishments. Eating out is fine and good, but not all the time. It is easy to develop spending habits that are wasteful keeping couples from experiencing a getaway weekend together. Sacrificing and cooking a small dinner together at home, in the ambiance of each other's presence, can be as exciting as going out on the town.

A Love Relationship by Design

From a practical position, a man who is truly a provider plans for the unexpected putting money aside to meet out of the ordinary or unexpected expenses that may occur. Common variables such as the miss management of means can lead to needs not being met. This takes us back to the definition of stewardship. The wisdom of the man and the woman, working together, will determine the success of the provision.

Be careful not to create unnecessary needs; for example, buying a two story house on a one story income. Just because you are approved to purchase the home does not mean that you can afford it. Meeting the monthly mortgage may not be a problem but paying taxes, homeowner fees, and maintenance may cause a burden. A need has now been created that strains the boundary of provision. Finding a solution to the now created problem regarding provision could mean picking up a second job. In turn, this takes away family time including your child's school functions and romance in the marriage.

Ecclesiastes 10:19 (NKJV) A feast is made for laughter, and wine makes merry; But money answers everything.

In context, when this bible verse states "money answers all things," it means it answers those things in which money is required. The number one problem

A Love Relationship by Design

among married couples is finances and many marriages are dissolved because of money matters. At times, lower levels of confidence, stress, and tension are the direct result from the lack of money. When bills are not met, emotions escalate, tensions rise, and two people who love each other are now at odds. Depending on the severity, this can be the beginning of how the enemy divides a house. Here is why? When money is absent, so can the absence of confidence, commitment and security. Amie Streater said "Statistics show that money problems cause marital strife more than any other issue. But I don't think it's for the reason that most people assume. I think it's all about sex. …..When money problems arise, many women have a really hard time having a sexual response. For women, safety and security are part of their languages of love. Women need to feel secure in order to relax and enjoy "quality time" with their husbands. In the middle of a financial crisis, sex is the last thing on many women's minds. For men it is different. Men require physical contact with their wives to feel loved, connected and okay in the world. To most men, there is no connection between the bank account and the bedroom." Women have an emotional response when they don't feel secure. This response can cause the man to feel rejected. In intimacy language, men desire sex as acceptance and women need a sense of security to provide it. In order for that to happen, there must be a bridge between a source for the two, and money answers that. Without this bridge, no one feels their needs are met and division seems to be inevitable. When money is available so is peace of mind. We can also look at this from a different angle, as some men's confidence is tied to their bank account and when it is depleted, so is he. Now, hopefully when you think of provision, you will realize money, at least in part, is an answer to the resolution that stabilizes the relationship.

    A true provider will make sacrifices for his family, but if not prudent, those sacrifices can create a need not being met somewhere else. This is why a man should not create unsustainable economic situations. When a man treats a woman a certain way she comes to expect it, so even if he can buy her things all the time he should balance it within reason. You may discover that eating a sandwich with each other at Subway™ can be far more invigorating than eating at a steakhouse and later stressing over the bill.

A Love Relationship by Design

Setting the Standards

Psalms 138:8 (NKJV) *"The Lord will perfect that which concerns me..."* This means God does not want second best for us. It's like waiting on a kidney transplant and the doctor saying we need a perfect match. The physician knows that anything less will not function properly and will minimize your chance for survival. God has your perfect match; however, it is our imperfections that make us perfect for each other. We are designed to make each other better. It simply means, don't force yourself into a relationship; allow God to bring one to you. He has a plan where your path will intersect with the one you are destined to be with. You just have to recognize and respond when it does.

Philippians 4:6 (NKJV) *"Be anxious for nothing, but in everything by prayer and supplication, with thanksgiving, let your requests be made known to God; and the peace of God, which surpasses all understanding, will guard your hearts and minds through Christ Jesus."*

Sometimes our human nature, our feelings or our loneliness can box us into relationships that God never ordained. Merely spending time with someone, to manage our anxieties, can lead to, *friends with benefits,* a relationship that falls outside of God's perfect will for us. It is not always these sexual inclusions, but temporary companionship and even romance, though innocent, where feelings can emerge.

Being anxious comes with a cost. You garner even more stress trying to remove yourself from a relationship that was never intended for you in the first place. Emotions, once in rhythm, can be like an earthquake; even after it is over you still feel the tremors. Timing and human intervention can result with us finding ourselves in the middle of life's predicaments, but most of our issues come directly from not seeking God first. Our affections and attractions can serve as blinders that keep us from seeing the true will of God. At times, we see only what we want to see. That is even when we know someone may not be right for us, we pursue them anyway. It is important to seek God before making any decisions, because the Word tells us that it is with prayer and supplication that we make our requests known to God with thanksgiving. Our confidence in Him begets thanksgiving, knowing that God will honor our prayers.

In fact, 1 John 5:14-15(NKJV) *"...now this is the confidence that we have in Him, that if we ask anything according to His will, He hears us. And if we know that He hears us, whatever we ask, we know that we have the petitions that we have asked of Him."*

A Love Relationship by Design

Evoking our own will can veer us away from His good and perfect will for us. We can ask God to bless us with the opportunity to meet someone compatible, but we must also request clarity to recognize and act on the opportunity when it arises.

I was awakened at 4:00am one morning to a startling epiphany. God revealed to me that of all the women that I had dated, hung out with and even pursued passionately, the results were always the same. They had all ended unsuccessfully in the area of a maturing relationship that would eventually lead to marriage. Some of the women that came into to my life were God sent and I am certain of that, but not for the reasons that I thought. We can easily misinterpret the reasons why individuals of the opposite sex enter our lives. They can appear for a reason, a season, or a lifetime.

There were others that I had invited into my life knowing full well they were not right for me. Our human nature tends to see our gender as the means of a possible connection even when it is not ordained by God, even though there may be commonalities or similar interests. We can feed on this when God's intention may have sent them there only to be an encouragement for a season.

A Love Relationship by Design

God's purpose for mankind is to experience His joy, which comes with the assurance that we have made a decision that is pleasing to Him. I would also like to note that a person can cross paths with their soul mate, but it may not be the right time to develop a union. We can become attracted to people who belong to someone else; tie souls intimately with someone who is not your soul mate. You can take a long relationship journey and even marry someone whom God never ordained for you. You can be at the altar saying "I do" and heavily questioning, "Am I doing the right thing?" Sometimes, either one or both people must mature before being ready for such a role. Seeking God before you make a move on your own can save you from added burdens that come from acting outside of God's perfect will.

If you and your partner are both believers, then you should have no problem holding hands and asking God to reveal why you crossed paths. If there is an objection from either party, yes, this includes you, then this could be a sign for you to exit.

> Matthew 18:19 (NKJV) *"Again I say to you that if two of you agree on earth concerning anything that they ask, it will be done for them by My Father in heaven."*

Set the standard by putting God first, even ahead of your own desires. But, if we make finding a mate a super spiritual event, we can miss God in His practical revelation. God gives us free will to either accept or reject his will. Relationships come down to human choice. God is not going to force anyone upon us, but will bring people across our paths that are *recognizably different or a perfectly right for you. It is like the old saying "you can lead a horse to the water, but you can't make it drink."* A man must prayerfully select the bride he believes God has blessed him with and to server his purpose. It is up to the bride to prayerfully accept and support that purpose.

She is the One…

*The one that when she enters the room
my spirit leaps with excitement knowing she is near.
You see my rib that was missing, she possesses it;
permeating the connection of our love atmosphere.
Time stops, and the calendar turns back the hand of time.
As I rewind in my mind,
a projection by which only God can define,
My queen, my helper,
she corresponds in purposeful necessity.
But not like a burden, because it is natural
(she is my rib) she rests in me.
The one that when I hurt she knows it,
when my wounds are open she closes it.
She knows when I smile whether are not it is real.
She authenticates if my affections are sincere,
or if I face an uncertain fear.*

A Love Relationship by Design

We are tied together by our soul, let's make that clear.
I have no interest in any other; she is my friend and my lover.
I was predestined to love only her, for I am her cover.
God knew what I needed before I even needed it.
He wrote and defined her DNA code and all that preceded it.
I can spot her out of crowd of ten million.
My faith supersedes my natural senses and reads into it.
We communicate on a level that exceeds expectation.
We speak to each other's Heart beyond human aspirations.
We are the elements that make up the glue.
We are the Wikipedia definition of duration.
We are full of passion; we have bridged our perceptions.
Purpose steers the credentials for our lives.
I love her as Christ loved the church,
the way God instructs men to love their wives..
because she is the one.

A Love Relationship by Design

Human Requirements

> "*There is a way that seems right to man but the end is destruction.*" Proverbs 14:12 (NKJV).

This passage refers to the lifestyles of the world. But it applies to us when we are tricked by our own perceptive understanding of ourselves and others. This can cause us to end up emotionally wounded and psychologically scared by the consequences of actions based on what felt right. In relationships, we depend on the law of natural progression. In terms of relationships, the law of natural progression is allowing those relationships to take a natural course. This natural course will ultimately determine whether or not the relationship is a natural fit by your normal actions and reactions. I see this as "go with the flow" methodology. It may be a good rule, but it is not without flaws. Remember, natural progression involves human action and we ourselves are flawed. We are like magnets and can either attract or become attracted to people whom deflate our value.

In a moment of emotional or passionate continuity, we can be deceived because it "feels right." Luther Ingram's song, *"If loving you is wrong, I don't want to be right,"* suggests that our humanity allows us to go down roads viewing life from a distorted perspective, based on our emotions. Usually, our initial reaction to one another sets the tone. To the man it may be visual and to the woman it may be a sense of security recognized through conversation. This often sets the natural progression into motion, but not everyone is always committed to moving forward. It Realize, this motion is motivated by human actions and responses , which are a mirror of our personality.

It is important to understand that we are attracted to people based on one's individual rules. These rules are the driver in a relationship because we are our own unique person. The natural law of progression is at work but under alternative influences. The idea of natural law of progression is the normal flow that creates an environment for the relationship to grow naturally. We often wonder why we have gone through multiple relationships, wasting valuable time and eventually discovering that there is a natural law of division at the end. This happens when something happens to disrupt this flow. Because each individual is governed by their own set of criteria, there has to be a merging of agreements for evolution to continue. Natural law of progression in conjunction with realistic aspirations lends itself to a better formula for success, we often discover that our expectations of each other under normal circumstances are not realistic. We look for perfection and that does not exist.

A Love Relationship by Design

The best way to explain the levels of importance is in the form of an upside down pyramid, consisting of physical, mental and spiritual attraction. The flow of continuity is based on what is most important to an individual. At the top, is **Physical Attraction. This is the** attraction to a person's physical attributes including their appearance, eyes, hair, height, body, to list a few and can be the main cause of a couple connecting. This is accompanied by the reaction to initial contact. You usually know on the first date whether there is an interest individually or collectively. At times, the odds are defied because pursuit is carried out in spite of the first impression.

The middle portion of the triangle is connecting on a *Mental and Emotional Attraction,* that is, understanding each other's feelings. In additional, one will generally see progress because of the ability to hold an intelligent conversation.

The tip of the upside down pyramid is *Spiritual Attraction,* defined as an attraction to someone based on their spiritual walk with God. More specific, as prescribed in this book, some attribute that describes one relationship with God through Jesus Christ. Unfortunately, our natural instinct is to be attracted to the external first. When in reality, we should first pray to God asking for direction to obtain a clear understanding of how we should relate to one another.

A Love Relationship by Design

When the pyramid is turned upright ***Spiritual Attraction*** is on top, ***Mental and Emotional Attraction*** is consistently at the center and ***Physical Attraction*** falls to the bottom. Consider for a moment the ramifications to a relationship when one or both of the participants disregard elements of attraction that bring balance to the relationship. Even elements of the relationship that once felt right, can go terribly wrong. Metaphorically speaking, the natural law of progression can be compared to deciding on a route along a rural road. It feels right; it is peaceful and the scenery is good. All is going well until you realize that you are lost and almost out of fuel only with no gas station in sight. When on your progressive road, it is a good idea to pull over, chart your progress, and make sure that provision has been made that will lead to a successful trip.

Significant situations and opportunities like the agreement of having children can bring a halt to fulfilling God's natural law of progression. Discussions of the unknown variables and potential areas of disagreement can prevent one from making that disastrous journey that ends in disappointment. Unemotional proceeding down the path is only good if you have an agreement on where you are to end up.

It all comes down to choices. We choose what we like and what will be tolerated. Choices are made when to enter into a relationship and when to walk away from potential situations. Our human imperfections can lead us to the end of a potentially good thing–both subjectively and objectively–with another person. From a one dimensional standpoint, our frayed version of life can catapult our disappointment unless we revise our perspective to viewing our lives from an aerial outlook.

> Proverbs 3:5-6 (NKJV) *"Trust in the LORD with all your heart, and lean not on your own understanding; in all your ways acknowledge Him, and He shall direct your paths."*

We cannot accomplish this on our own. God's guidance is essential to our success.

> God also said, *"I will instruct you and teach you in the way you should go; I will guide you with my eye…"* Psalm 32:8 (NKJV).

When we determine that there is no need for God's help in our relationships, then we are prone to failure. Fear is another key factor that can lead us down the road to failure. When a man begins to possess deep desires for a woman and the relationship begins to take the couple into areas where the woman perceives vulnerability, she may become scared. This can lead to her withdrawal or retreat in an effort to put distance in the relationship until she can consider all the unknowns and be more certain of the relationship. This may also be true of the male. It is not that the components of natural flow aren't accessible; it simply means you are in unfamiliar territory. Depending on the severity, it can be normal to feel this way, but is extremely important that the couple share these feelings with their partner making certain that both individuals are in step on this relationship journey.

I cannot stress enough how important it is to trust God and pray together for confirmation and revelation that your relationship be intended for marriage. Please, do not rush into any decisions until you receive the word from God. Confirmation and revelation are not found in chirping of birds, signs miraculously appearing in the clouds, or some prophesy telling you God ordained it. If He pleases, God is capable of these feats as he has used a talking donkey as well as many other animals and miraculous signs to deliver his messages. But you can completely and entirely depend on the fact that God deals with each of us based on how our understanding of Him. The confirmation usually comes from the peace and calm of God resting on the marriage couple along with His revelation through their communion with one another that assures the relationship was meant to be. This simply translates in both firming believing that they are right for each other.

Amos 3:3 (NKJV) asks, *"Can two walk together, except they be agreed?"*

A Love Relationship by Design

This application applies in multiple phases of life, not just marriage, and is a major component in building rock strong foundations. It does not merely mean that we will agree on everything but considers that we strive toward a place whereby we can agree.

The word "agree" is from the Greek word "*sumphoneo*" which means to "sound together." Perceive your agreement as a symphony which has different instruments playing together at the same time. Though the instruments differ, like the man and woman, the objective is the same; make beautiful music. In a symphony, each instrument complements the other and the final product is the sound is complete. This is the same in relationships. What each individual brings to the relationship should complement the other and together they will form completeness.

It is extremely important not to begin a relationship with the idea of changing the other individual. You should begin by finding a person that matches your desires, instead of believing that you can change or that your mate will change after you are married. Keep in mind that each person is uniquely different, but can share a common bond. It is important not to try to change anyone because many times one of the following two result happen. You spend a lot of time attempting to change the person, and when they don't adhere to your wishes, you become frustrated and disappointed not only because of the time you have wasted but because you don't understand why the other person does not realize that you were just trying to make them better. If they do change, they can lose their individuality and become someone they are not meant to be, and they become disappointed, obstinate and angry. In order for real changes to happen, one must be willing to make them on their own.

It is important that you begin on a solid foundation. Your faith is that foundation. The Bible instructs us not to be "unequally yoked with unbelievers." (2 Corinthians 6:14). Yoke-like agreement is pivotal in determining the direction of a relationship. -

A Love Relationship by Design

An Unequal Yoke Drives Perception

In third world countries, it is still common to see beasts of burden like oxen bound by a wooden yoke. This forces them to walk in step with each other. Often, there is a basket attached on each end of the yoke where something is carried. One end may contain water, and the other end grain, but if the weight shifts to one side, then that side carries more of the burden.

Relationships can be unequally yoked as well. This may be true when one person in the relationship carries all the financial, decision making, or conversational weight, to name a few. Over a period of time, that relationship will become a burden to the weight bearer. If a person holds a glass of water for a few minutes, it's not a problem, but let that person hold the same glass of water for a few hours, and it is sure to become a burden. It is not necessarily the weight, but how long one carries it. The amount of patience an individual possesses can differ, but eventually it becomes easier to unload the burden then it is to continue carrying it around.

Christian marriages are ending in divorce at about the same rate as non-Christian marriages. It is

A Love Relationship by Design

amazing that the same people, who once loved each other so much and hated being apart, now can't stand to be around each other. It is not the agreement that is the issue, but the disagreements unresolved that divide the harmony. At times, you have to create a storm, in order to calm them. This simply means when it comes to your feelings, be honest with your mate, even if it hurts. To keep the slate clean, you have to face the truth, resolve it, and leave it in the past. Often, we discover that the other individual never knew how we were feeling because we never mentioned what was bothering us.

In the beginning of relationships, be cognizance of the signs and indicators that are evident when two people are not equally yoked. Avoiding these issues and thinking they will work themselves out, will only make your future suspect. No relationship is perfect and all require work, so by acknowledging their differences, couples creates an atmosphere whereby they agrees on issues that need work. When couples learn to work through their differences, it signifies that they have the ability to be in harmony together in the midst of distraction.

I have a Christian friend from Nigeria who is in an arranged marriage. In America, we have the freedom to select who we will marry, but often it is to our advantage and we should consider the opinions of our family and friends regarding our relationships. They can

A Love Relationship by Design

often discern what we refuse to see or are too blind to consider. However, listening to or depending on the opinions of others can be dangerous if their advice comes from the wrong motivation. When the opinion of others drives your relationship, it indicates that a strong infrastructure does not exist. We are instructed to seek sound advice from time to time, but when is not sound it could further complicate matters.

 Sometimes our freedom is our proverbial thorn in the flesh, because just as easily as we choose to enter a relationship, we can just as easily exit a relationship without ever giving it a fair chance to survive. In western culture, we consult everyone concerning relationship problems and issues ending up with a lot of opinions and ungodly advice from people who are in wrecked relationships themselves. What I admire most about my friend from Nigeria is that he does not spread their personal business around. It is a private matter. If he has an issue with his wife, he speaks with her parents, not his own, and she vice versa. This prevents any biased actions.

A Love Relationship by Design

Change Management

When a relationship is dissolved, it is usually never instant but progressive. There are certain factors that gradually eat away at it until it becomes a burden viewed as no longer worth carrying. At the end, we can find ourselves pointing a finger at the other as the root cause. Even in our self-proclaimed perfection, we all play a role in our relationship's demise. Even when we claim to have done nothing to cause the other person's behavior, we can be a reason that the relationship failed.

Cheating or abuse is not good for building a relationship, and the victim must be strong enough to not allow it. If there are no consequences or repercussions to these acts, then the perpetrator becomes comfortable enough to believe that they got away with it once, so they can continue doing it again and again. The truth is every relationship needs balance, and when this element is not present, the relationship will eventually collapse. Balance simply means there must be enough variables, that no one thing or even person rules everything. Like gravity, when in a relationship, we need to be the balance for each other that will help us stay grounded. This keeps one person from dominating the relationship or leaving the other feeling oppressed or unable to equally express their ideas and opinions. We

A Love Relationship by Design

need to afford our spouse the right to challenge any of our behaviors and actions that are unhealthy for a successful relationship or our personal well-being.

Today, how an average man or woman views their roles in a relationship is plagued with an incorrect thought processes handed down through the generations that is inconsistent with God's truth. When a person accepts thoughts or perceptions that are not in line with God's word, these misconceptions become a handicap to the mind. We become a prisoner of our own thoughts. Each person must first look within their own heart before they look at their partner in judgment. Matthew 3-5 (NKJV)[3] "And why do you look at the speck in your brother's eye, but do not consider the plank in your own eye? [4] Or how can you say to your brother, 'Let me remove the speck from your eye'; and look, a plank *is* in your own eye? [5] Hypocrite! First remove the plank from your own eye, and then you will see clearly to remove the speck from your brother's eye." When being completely honest with yourself, you will realize that there is a life time of revising your own imperfections and shortcomings.

Some personal views need to change, because they are founded in the desire to change the other person in the relationship to be more similar to them. The reality is that we were each purposely made different and our life path mold us in our own individuality. You

A Love Relationship by Design

have to become selfless and understand that the others view is just as important as your view. In addition men and women are different. These differing designs require differing personalities. We operate at an optimum when we operate as ourselves, un-imitated. Change is relevant when people change ways that are toxic to the relationship.

We often hear couples complain that their partner had changed from the person they once were. More than likely, this is a true statement. We all change as trends, styles and even our views are altered. People are refined physically and mentally. As individuals mature in their faith, they are even transformed spiritually. A friend of mine offered an analogy of how a relationship is very similar to a road trip; one has to keep refueling. When you don't stop to refuel, you run out of gas and your passenger begins to question your judgment and mental fortitude.

How you view these changes are based on your experiences that can alter your perception on certain aspects of life. An instance is when we first meet our mate, they may seem perfect but later, little by little, we begin to see flaws or holes in their cape. Depending on the severity of the flaws, your behavior may become reflective of the changed view of that person. The truth is, none of us is perfect. We must consider that what we are really seeing is our partner without the veil of

A Love Relationship by Design

infatuation placed by us. God's Word makes it perfectly clear that we are to love, adapt and forgive each other even when it's hard. Remembering that we are created to be helpmates to our spouses, the character traits that both possess, good and bad,, work together to bring balance of character as we become one.

It is human nature to protect each other's feelings. For a period of time, we may harbor our own true emotion to spare undue burdens on our spouse. A good example of this concept is; a wife has been told by her husband that he feels stagnate in his job. He is frustrated due to lack of advancement in his career. Meanwhile, the wife hates her job also, but keeps this information concealed from her husband because she doesn't want cause extra burden on him when he is already concerned with his own career. Without each other being aware of the other's thoughts, her views about work are changing and his contentment with his job is changing. They are both changing in some respect but neither one is aware of it.

I work for a company that uses technology for directional drilling. This means we can set up a drilling rig in one location and be drilling a half mile down the road where it was impossible to place the rig. When we are comfortable enough to communicate freely without scrutinizing each other, we too can take a directional approach to address a situation that is difficult and

A Love Relationship by Design

would normally be avoided; and by doing so, you are allowing the conversation to arrive at the focus of the actual problem by means other than direct confrontation that can cause more friction and potential hurt—making it impossible to address.

Most relationships experience what is known as the drifting process. A drifting can happened over time when couples take each other for granted and become bored with the current status. -In this process there could be a gradual change in attitude, opinion and position. Although common and expected, it must be recognized and attended to; otherwise, a couple is destined to drift apart. A Common phrase heard is, "…we have grown apart or we have nothing in common anymore," or even worse, "I love you, or I care for you, but I'm just not *in* love with you anymore." Dishonesty, lack of communication and failure to adjust to normal changes can add to the strife driving a wedge between any couple. Some people get bored quickly and that can lead to drifting apart as a means of creating an exit. They create excuses not to see each other communication decelerates and everything that supports the relationship begins to fade. Be careful because drifting apart and then connecting to another person can lead to infidelity. The drifting process is synonymous with avoidance because it kills the atmosphere that keeps the relationship chemistry alive.

A Love Relationship by Design

When an individual reaches their limit, then any single insignificant incident can cause a major drift in their relationship. It is called the breaking point. The media is not a help. Society now breeds a philosophy that has diminished our strengths. My grandparents were married for 74 years; they had tough skin because they stood up against those events that would break us today. Now people separate over just about anything, like turning the toilet paper the wrong way. Media billboards are plastered with the message that you can get a divorce in 24 hours implying that divorce is glorified as the norm. So, do you go with the norm or do you push against the grain and exercise the patience to work together in opposition of the drift?

The list is endless; a change of careers, giving birth, midlife crisis, school, menopause are all contributors. If you experience drift that is out of control while simultaneously being pulled emotionally toward an outside person who relates to your situation, you can be pulled into a state of confusion. I consider this type of situation to be the feeding ground of infidelity. It could be possible for a man and woman to grow weary in the relationship at the same time. It is also possible for them to drift apart without any effort on either part to address that issue. With other daily life priorities in play much time could pass without any of them acknowledging it as a pertinent issue until it is seemingly too late. -

A Love Relationship by Design

Learn to manage the drift because if you jump from one relationship to another based on this isolated definition, you will be forever changing into a different person. Pray together as a couple along with applying action of renewal, for faith without works is dead.

Spontaneous Diversification- creating spark through different means. In order to defy the odds of boredom you must not be too redundant in your actions because those once exciting moments can quickly become dull and stale. I once worked on a government funded program that was geared to help educate and bring awareness to the community about substance abuse. One of the interesting facets of drug addiction is that the addict uses the drug in an attempt to obtain a high that one's body cannot biologically or chemically ever reproduce. For the addict, the first experience was new and thereby exciting, but after being exposed to the substance he cannot get a high that equals that first time experience. In relationships, this same type of experience gives way to a loss of interest. When I was married, eating at the same restaurant and bowling became second nature for our entrainment. We did it so often that we developed and immunity to certain foods and bowling. Science has proven that having too much of a food once love by a person in turn can make them hate that same food. It is not that bowling and eating out were not great activities; it just means there should have been variety and other interests creating balance.

A Love Relationship by Design

When you diversify your recreational habits, it allows you the opportunity to undertake activities that you have not participated in for a while and now can actually get excited about doing them again. It always a good idea to make a list of those activities that you enjoy doing but also consider things that you thought you might not ever enjoy and try them. Sometimes the activities you thought you wouldn't like become a favorite while some of the interests you used to enjoy, you have now outgrown. Little sparks add adventure and excitement to your relationship. You begin to look forward to doing things with your partners again.

When money is tight, you can improvise by doing activities that cost little or no money. Try something like this: drive near an airport as close as possible to where planes are taking off; then look at each other and come up with a financial plan for your next trip together. Now you have something to build toward providing quality time together. To add to the experience, listen to quiet music in the background and use your imagination. Share your hopes and dreams with your partner. This is a perfect way to draw closer together and to gain a better understanding of the one you love the most.

It is common for relationships to be spontaneous in one area while dead in another. Often, married individuals reminisce on former people they once dated

A Love Relationship by Design

focusing on that special characteristic they enjoyed or that one grand moment that they shared, romanticizing a relationship that no longer exists. It is not uncommon for someone to hold similar feelings toward more than one of their old relationships. By entertaining these thoughts, one has actually shepherd that old flame into the center of their current relationship. Realistically, it can take the very best of three to four people to make a perfect mate. Most of the time, each possess characteristics you desire along with others you do not. No one person is perfect but traits can be acquired that will make anyone more rounded.

Intellectually, consider attending a symphony or opera if you have never been. *Physically*, try doing different things together, like add cultural mix for diversity, or begin working out if that is not the norm for you. Reach outside of the box and discover what life has to offer. *Spiritually*, seek to gain a closer relationship with your Creator. Use your creative inspirations to cause sparks keeping the flames from going out on your love life.

A Love Relationship by Design

Checks and Balances

According to WikiAnswers.com the concept of "*Checks and Balances*" comes from the American Constitution. The different branches of the government "check" each other's power so that no one branch has more power than the other. When two adults are able to discuss matters of the heart and come up with a viable solution, it says one partner is no greater than the other. When the bible states submit one to another, these words means to recognize the other person's rank. This command is good and can prevent each other from misusing one's power to monopolize and or dominate situations with gender formalities.

When it comes to the sexes, both have proven to have made good and bad choices. When we bounce information off each other it allows us to view life from different angles. Sometimes without that special mate in your life keeping you grounded you have freedom to roam into forbidden areas. In freedom there can be a sense of captivity. God knows us better than we know ourselves. Looking into the mirror we see our frontal image but are blinded to the back. God sees what we cannot and, at times, positions the right person in our life to help us see these blind spots. When you begin to see the value added by that person, what once appeared

A Love Relationship by Design

to be a nagging wife is actually the one that forced you to rethink the choices you were about to make.

During these rough economic times, every financial decision can impact another. You purchase expensive outfits that cost $200.00 without notifying your spouse, so tensions rise. You argue that your spouse is trying to control you. This may not be the issue at all. It could be that your spouse knew where the sales were and could have gotten you three outfits from quality clothing lines at a much lesser cost. Communication in this scenario could have reduced the drama and saved money. Have you ever stepped back and thoughtfully asked your spouse why you were being questioned? God gives us what we need but not always what we want. The people who he places in our life are not always going to agree with us because their purpose is to tell us the truth even when it hurts. Those people who challenge us are not necessarily trying to be controversial, but generally have our best interest at heart. We must revise our views so we can see those truths that we have apparently hidden from ourselves.

A Love Relationship by Design

Actions and Reactions

Isaac Newton once said that for every action there is an equal and opposite reaction. Men and women both react, we just most often react differently. Much exhaustion can surface from how men and women respond to each other when issues arise. Each believes the other is unreasonable and selfish in their demeanor and cannot logically understand why the other just doesn't comprehend. This sounds familiar in your personal life doesn't it? Men have the tendency to resolve matters within himself while his helpmate, the woman, feels shut when not included. She responds in this manner out of purpose. She desires to help, yet the male ego tells him he can handle everything on his own. In humility, he attempts to resolve it so as not to burden her. She begins to feel rejected because he won't talk. Both spouses believe they are doing the right thing but are becoming disconnected in the process. This is when the woman argues that the man is hormonal, because she clearly recognizes a shift in his moods.

Meanwhile the woman is analytical attempting to figure out what is wrong with her man. She then begins to consistently probe and he concludes she is nagging. At this point, they both become extremely frustrated with one other. She tries to help, which from her

A Love Relationship by Design

position is noble, but believes that she just will not back away. Tensions begin to rise and a real argument can pursue. If only, they had just talked about the situation, it could have already been resolved. The result is now an unnecessary affliction. No one means harm, yet both are hurt.

When a man withdraws to himself, he is one dimensional. This one issue can completely shut him down and totally consume him. In some ways, this is why a man who cheats becomes distant. This does not mean that a just because a man is distant that he is cheating. It simply states that something has his mind. He cannot grant a woman his undivided attention because his thoughts are scattered. In this case, a man does not ordinarily possess a multitask personality. This is not necessarily bad because, if used properly, he can finish one burden before moving on to the next. This is another reason why God provided him a helpmate. While a man may need to accomplish one thing at a time, the woman needs her attention and will intuitively detect there is something wrong. Typically men typically want to be in control and when believing he is not he becomes closed off, as if a mechanism commences to protect and shield him from outside interference. What he does not realize is that he cannot close doors to the people he love and yet expect them to love him the same. Men feel a need for space to breathe when faced with complex issues. They try to rationalize

A Love Relationship by Design

their options on their own. This is a dangerous game because when others try to help, men feel pressured and become defensive. Their ego poses a threat against them because they are 'the men' or 'the heads'. They are vertically in park until they resolve it. This means he feels less than a man if he can't figure it out, not realizing the woman is there to help him in the process.

This one issue, no matter how minor, can affect a string of others. His wife begins believing that she has done something wrong when in fact she has not. By now, her imagination is going wild analyzing his every move. She can easily assume that there is someone else. His family time is compromised by his thoughts. He begins spending more time in recreational activities like basketball and golf to think through his thoughts. He then spends less time with his spouse and talks less. This does not mean he does not love her, but typically, he cannot accomplish two things at once. Often a man believes that what the woman wants is to be able to respect and follow her husband, so if he does not have it all together it only adds to the burden. In turn, he will diligently attempt to get it together so that they may communicate with confidence.

The woman on the other hand needs affection and attention. These two seemingly simple actions are more complex that they seem. They engulf a myriad of considerations that fit into these actions. Her receiving

A Love Relationship by Design

the attention that she requires can be simplified by him simply opening up to her. His issues do not negate her needs. In fact, by just letting her in, may satisfy the need because, by nature, she desires to help. She thrives on intellectual conversation, for the most part. She wants to talk and also wants to listen, and in this endeavor she can also be consumed with a thought of a different nature. The major difference is the woman knows how to multi-task, but also retain all that occurs in the relationship. Remember, the they are the multiplier and so is everything about them. A man can go along thinking everything is alright but the woman will remind him five years later that it is not. One failed commitment can leave a blemished record forever. His not being considerate of her is the biggest issue. She doesn't mind following a man of his word but will forever question him if his actions are not consistent. She wants to see actions more than simply hearing it. She wants to be affirmed and admired but mainly she desires to be a part of his thoughts, intentions, and most importantly a part of his life. When she is shut out, she interprets it as rejection. If you don't address it, she just might be singing Fantasia's song *"If you don't want me then don't talk to me, so go ahead and free yourself."*

A Love Relationship by Design

Communication Eliminates Perception

Proverbs 15:1 (NKJV) *"A soft answer turns away wrath, But a harsh word stirs up anger."*

When we analyze relationships, it is not just merely communication but more so how we communicate. There is such a thing as bad communication, especially when you do it in a demeaning and demoralizing manner. When you curse at each other, verbally abuse or tear the other person down, it usually result in both people saying things that stir up anger. The truth of the manner is there are some things you say that are forever etched in a person's mind, and those words can't be taken back or erased. It is important to note that when you address each other with respect, you generally get the same in return. Because you are one with each other, the hurt communicated is an affliction onto yourself.

*"When things are out of balance nothing
is what it appears to be,
Chaos seems to be in constant rotation
causing everything around to begin spiraling.
The wrong words at the wrong time,
the wrong thoughts from the wrong mind
The open mouth causes a bind,
and two misunderstood people
become the fracture underlined."*

A Love Relationship by Design

We as people change but, the fact remains, people's perception of us sometimes never does. In relation to man and woman, what one says and what the other hears may be totally different, but when you communicate clearly it erases the line one could be trying to read between. Attempting to read the other's mind can cause you to misinterpret what truly exists. There is a gender difference, but beyond that, women are more emotional, while men tend to be more physical, in general. Men are less emotional, but emotional none the less. Most often, men tend to hide their emotions. Let me offer a scenario where a man and woman having different, possibly even false, perceptions are engaged in the same event: They go on a first date; While sitting and chatting, the man is clueless because the woman is smiling and engaged in the conversation. He is attracted to her and is saying to himself, "Give me a couple of days, and I am going to have her." On the other hand, the woman is smiling to keep from laughing in utter disappointment. She is saying to herself, "God, I should have listened and been patient. Get me out of this situation. I will get my free dinner and drink, and I hope he loses my number." These two people are in the same situation, but their perceptions are totally different.

When a woman says she is looking for a good man it has to be decoded or translated. A good man to her is one with expanded options. She is looking for a spiritual man with Godly principles. He can be nice but

A Love Relationship by Design

must be confident. He cannot exhibit a behavior that is timid or be intimidated by the woman. No matter what you think men, a woman doesn't want someone she can run over or control. At first, it may appear as if she does but she will soon become bored. She wants someone who has opinions even if those opinions differ from hers. It is a plus when the man can challenge her choices and thinking, especially if she believes his position will make her better. She may challenge him, at times but is ecstatic that she has a man who does not let her have her way all the time. These actions provide the woman with the security whereby she can trust the man enough to follow him. In the long run, the woman is seeking a leader because her true desire is to follow.

    This is much the reason why the seemingly good guys, who are too passive, appear to get passed up. So in essence just being a good guy is not enough. You must be able to set the tone for a lifelong song and dance. Essentially a man has to "Man Up"; be consistent, decisive, and know what he wants. One must be able to take control of situations when it is required. On occasion, we have all noticed "good girls" with "bad boys." This phenomenon is because the man possesses the confidence to transgress against the norm. A woman desires a man who knows who he is, what he wants and believes in himself even when no one else does. On the other hand, what a man looks for in a good woman is generally a lot more simplistic. Most likely, he just

A Love Relationship by Design

wants to be respected as a man. A man's home is his refuge. After a day of taking life's beatings, the last thing that he wants is to come home and get beat up with attitude and drama. He desires are for a woman who is there for him, bandages his wounds and encourages him to keep fighting a good fight. This is especially true when the man depends on her support. He desires a woman who is tuned in to his needs and has no issue fulfilling those desires. In addition, he adores a woman who is a great mother and keeper of her home. With these characteristics evident, a man believes that he possesses a woman worth keeping.

Now imagine this scenario. Every night before going to bed, you grab your spouse by the hand and with no music playing, you embrace and dance closely. No one is saying a word, but intense communication is taking place. This is non-verbal communication. The man is saying, "I need you," and the woman is saying, "I feel loved." If not more so, non-verbal communication is just as important as verbal communication. Remember, how you communicate can and will leave room for error if the communication is not clear.

When a man is with his spouse and always frowning and appearing distant, to her it may communicate that he is unhappy with her has met someone else that is consuming his thoughts. But instead the man is only frustrated and frowning because

A Love Relationship by Design

he's not happy with his job and feels less than a man because he wants to give her more. If it is not communicated clearly, this perceived moment will lead to dissension and resentment.

    Women maximize communication while most men minimize it. This leaves a disparity between the two. According to a bestselling book, "The Female Brain" by Lou Ann Brizendine, women speak 20,000 words a day compared to the average man 7,000. Clearly, this is proof of the talkative women and the silent men, so how can people bridge the communication gap? Perceptions are drawn from the lack of formal knowledge of the other person. A good example of this is delivering your fiend, out of kindness, a seafood platter from your favorite restaurant only to discover that they are allergic to seafood. It was a nice gesture but it did not accomplish anything positive? Do not leave anything open to perception. We all have our idiosyncrasies but must consider mitigating how we deal with our differences based on understanding each other. Men, when a woman wants to talk about an issue that she's going through, it is wise to ask her if she wants you to help or simply listen. Sometimes, If you try to guess and are wrong, your response can cause more harm than good.

    Relationships are built on communication and are destroyed because of the lack of it. Verbal and non-verbal communications are only effective when they are used collectively. Never leave anything up to perception. We are each wired a little differently, and false impressions can be made due to a lack of candid and open conversation. In an argument, when a woman says, "Don't worry about it; it's over," in reality this means you had better worry about it because it is far from over! Remember she reciprocates and multiplies. Men often hope, and sometimes actually believe, that situations will just go away and resolve themselves. Women, on the other hand, will continue with their daily functions, but later on that same issue will rise to the surface again.

      This is why communication is imperative to the vitality of a successful union. Practical reasoning and intuition can be distorted by heightened emotion and, at times, blurred judgments. In these instances, decisions are made irrationally, rather than logically. Sometimes the figments of our imaginations will create the biggest burdens. Communication can be said to be the life of the party but it is also the life of the relationship.

Purpose

Purpose

To accept the call to which I heard,
God unveiled the power of His Word.
God bridged the continuum between time and space,
He moved me swiftly into my destined place.

When it comes to purpose one thing is clear. Our purpose is to glorify God in everything we do. Through the revision process this is our goal.

> Philippians 3:13,14 (NKJV) *"Brethren, I do not count myself to have apprehended; but one thing I do, forgetting those things which are behind and reaching forward to those things which are ahead, I press toward the goal for the prize of the upward call of God in Christ Jesus."*

As we progress in our spiritual walk with God, we should become more and more like Him. We are being transformed into the likeness of God, changed from our old way of living. It is through this growth that we can lead lives that glorify God.

It is imperative to ask yourself this question; "Do I glorify God in the way I treat my spouse?" It certainly does not glorify Him if you cheat or mistreat the one you are supposed to love. How we treat one another is an expansion of our maturity. When we do not grow, our behaviors remain the same. Beyond living a life that pleases God, we are to help transform the lives of others through the gifts and abilities of our spouse. When our purpose is in sync with those of our spouse we become more effective in what God has called us to do.

A Love Relationship by Design

Purpose of Union

Mark 10:9 (NKJV) *"...therefore, what God has joined together let no man separate."*

This scripture is clear, so the question begs of who has joined you together. We often build relationships without God's advice, direction or guidance, and consequently, they fail. We all have a purpose, but it becomes useless when we are distracted. Sometimes a relationship can become distracted. We build relationships on sex, amenity or convenience and they generally fade as quickly as they began. When God places people in each other's life, there is a purpose and a reason they are together. In our directives of achieving a yoked equality; the development of passions; and understanding the reality of our own perceptions, we realize there is something greater at stake.

Something unique was placed in you before you were even born and that uniqueness supplements the very essence of your union. A process proceeded with purpose, assures that the relationship is not merely for each other, but is for Him. Our human response of love, passion, and concern for one another is the natural outcome in the process of glorifying Him and we receive enjoy from each other as an added benefit.

A Love Relationship by Design

When one truly matures in their faith, divorce is not an option or issue as one learns to control their emotions and feelings. Realized or not, when those vital pieces we each possess individually are placed together, we as a whole can move nations and change worlds. When you realize your marriage is not about you, but for the glory of God and what He desires to accomplish through you as a couple, then God's purpose for your marriage can and will be fulfilled.

> Romans 8:28-30 (NKJV) *"And we know that all things work together for good to those who love God, to those who are the called according to His purpose. For whom He foreknew, He also predestined to be conformed to the image of His Son, that He might be the firstborn among many brethren. Moreover whom He predestined, these He also called; whom He called, these He also justified; and whom He justified, these He also glorified."*

Sometimes, revision is captured through the redirecting and rerouting of our lives. We are detoured on the streets of life by circumstances that we did not plan, but God's GPS allows us to navigate these circumstances and uncharted routes.

In the Old Testament, Joseph was redirected by way of dreams to reunite with his family. Similarly,

A Love Relationship by Design

Jonah, who was recognized in 2 Kings as a servant and a prophet, was rerouted through the belly of a fish after attempting to escape the plan and purpose of God. In the New Testament, Jesus was rerouted to Egypt as a baby to keep him from King Herod's order of death. Likewise, Paul was redirected while sailing to Bethesda to ensure that God's purpose was fulfilled to the West.

Arriving to your destination is not always a comfortable journey. I can imagine it was extremely uncomfortable for Jonah in the belly of a fish. Likewise, tyranny, heartbreaks, lost jobs, and failed marriages all have a way of changing our direction and course. It may not appear so at the time, but God is moving you to your destiny through what appears to be an alternate route. In Jonah's case, God proved that he could preach change to those Jonah considered unchangeable. At times, the revisions are not what God can bring to you, but what He can do through you.

> Ecclesiastes 3:1 (NKJV) *"To everything there is a season, and a time to every purpose under the heaven."*

You should pursue your purpose as though your very breath depends on it. God's plan for the original man was to work or cultivate the Garden of Eden and protect it. Today, man is still created with a purpose. That purpose is to cultivate the God given gifts so that God receives glory out of man's life. Not everyone is a preacher, but your talents, abilities, and crafts can be a ministry. Whether you are working in a lawn business or corporate America, your life can be a beacon that draws others to Christ. As you learn to use the abilities that God has given you, He expands your territory.

A Love Relationship by Design

Man as Priest

Men are to function as priest in their home. One of the responsibilities of the priest in the Old Testament was to offer sacrifices. This act atoned for the sins of the people. One primary purposes of the priest was to keep himself clean of sin. This is not to say he is perfect, but his conduct, character, and conversation must be pleasing to God. He is the representative of his family as well as the people of his community. Remember, he is held accountable for that he was given stewardship over. Living a life separate from the world presents his priestly features. Although Romans is speaking to all Christians in general…

> Romans 12:1-2 (NKJV) *"I beseech you therefore, brethren, by the mercies of God, that you present your bodies a living sacrifice, holy, acceptable to God, which is your reasonable service. And do not be conformed to this world, but be transformed by the renewing of your mind, that you may prove what is that good and acceptable and perfect will of God."*

As priest of the home, it starts with how you love your wife, especially in front of your children. Your life becomes the representation of how to live and love.

A Love Relationship by Design

Anyone can be a husband, not every man is a priest. When a man cheats or mistreats his wife, whether physical or mental, he indicates that he is not functioning as priest.

Moreover, a husband's prayer life covers his family because he goes to God on their behalf. Typically, we find that the woman is often the prayer warrior of the family, but the man should go before God daily covering his family in prayer. When the man fails to uphold his priestly duties, the enemy slithers through the small crack in the armor to divide the house.

> Mark 3:27 (NKJV) *"No one can enter a strong man's house and plunder his goods, unless he first binds the strong man. And then he will plunder his house."*

When the man develops a consistent, fervent prayer life his family becomes strong and able to reject temptation. The purpose of the enemy is to keep the man from praying. Consistent prayer life also allows a man the ability to offer guidance for his family. As the priest, he must be open to teaching so that he can also be a teacher in his home. This means he must stand on God's Word as the foundation for family guidance. Taking the time to share the word of God with his family, keeps them in one accord, in sync. This does not mean the man knows everything, but it does indicate that he understands the standard that he must set for his family. Often, the woman of the family has more knowledge of the scriptures, but the man's willingness to study and grow so that his family is grounded and can grow is the sign of a true priest.

A Love Relationship by Design

Purpose of a Helpmate

God put man to sleep and took his rib and made a woman and for him, a suitable helpmate.

I Corinthians 11:9 (NKJV) *"Neither was man not created for woman, but woman for man."*

If a woman loves you and you inform her of your vision, she will process it and instantly attempt to multiply it. A woman always gives back more than she is given. This can be either good or bad. In the case of Eve, Satan went to her instead of Adam, because he knew by nature that she would multiply, meaning that she would see more than it really was. He knew that the idea of being similar to God, knowing good and evil, would appeal to her emotions.

If she sees and understands, a woman will attempt to birth a man's vision. She will labor and research making sure that he is successful. This is her nature.

When God promised Abraham a child, for good or bad, mostly bad, Sarah went and found Hagar the handmaiden to make it happen. In a related story, my father is a pastor and every time there is an anniversary celebration for him, my mom works relentlessly behind the scenes, literally all night, to make sure the program a success. This dedication is in no way for a part of the reward, but by human nature, she multiplies the seed. If the woman in a man's life is smarter than he or handles finances better, he is not to panic. She is an asset that simply makes him better. She complements him making his goals and purpose attainable. God places you in the circle of the right people to help fulfill your purpose. The problem with some people is that they perceive the need to do it all themselves. Delegate the work according to the strengths of those on your team. That means you must be aware of what treasures they possess and entrust the corresponding obligations and responsibilities to them. God said it is not good for man to be alone (Genesis 2:18). Although it is not good for man to be alone, he is, at times, required to spend time alone with God. He must be careful not remain alone too long because his biological and physiological makeup could pose a threat to himself. This means the flesh can become an obstacle that leads to sexual misconduct.

Our physical nature makes us vulnerable to pending desires and affections. Today, it is not uncommon for relationship avoidance to take precedence over commitment. We sometimes hide behind work, kids, and even our spirituality as reasons why we do not have time for companionship. We have compromised our integrity to a substandard way of thinking. The carnal man, working outside of God's

A Love Relationship by Design

creative purpose for the proper dating relationship, has invented what the world calls, "friends with benefits". This substitutes the perfect intent of why God created woman for man in the first place. Because patience is rare, so is the tolerance to contend with the ups and downs of a love life as it plays out in a long reality series.

My Queen

*He who finds a wife finds a good thing
and obtains favor of the Lord.*

*A man must understand his purpose and
this woman would complement the man of God.*

*God's favor is through the woman
for whatever seed the man plants in her
She naturally multiplies it, gives it life,
and gives it back to him in abundance.*

*Men, be careful what you give her…
honor her, for she is your facilitator, incubator,
and your lifelong accentuator.*

*If you treasure her, she would extend herself
to make sure you are on an upward elevator.*

*She will fight for you,
and keep your back.*

She will wholeheartedly defend you

A Love Relationship by Design

when your character is under attack.

*She is a reciprocator; she is multi-tasked
be careful what you give her.*

*Men, you must be warned...
there is nothing worse
then a woman scorned!*

*Take care of her,
For she is your Queen.*

*By all inclination, she is vital
in the fulfilling your dreams.*

*Sow God's word in her,
she will be a mansion with open doors.*

*And, as the king of that castle,
you will certainly get yours.*

*Take your pride and deactivate,
Bend your knees and meditate.*

*Embrace your baby and celebrate!
You have a Proverbs 31 woman.*

*A God-joined marriage to dedicate
She is looking for a man with direction.*

*Who gives their children correction,
and provides family protection?*

A Love Relationship by Design

*Be careful what you give her,
give her affection. She is first next to Christ,
she is not some average woman,
she is your wife.*

*She is delicate like a flower,
but she will be strong at adversity's hour.*

*She will be like a strong tower…
So be careful what you give her.*

*She will speak life back into you,
from the same breath God originally blew
that gave her life.*

*She is not a woman you degrade,
She is a Queen, and she is your wife.*

*She is a nurturer, with a sixth sense.
She reads outside of the box with intuitive evidence.
She requires a listening ear,
a man who is strong and sincere.*

*A man who embraces and holds her,
makes her laugh and consoles her.*

*The way you treat her makes her trust you.
your love upholds her,
So love her as Christ loved the church.*

*That means you would literally die for her.
She **is** you, and you are one.*

A Love Relationship by Design

Be careful what you give her.
Pray for her,
and she will abundantly pray for you.

Stand by her side,
and she will certainly stand with you.

Give her gifts.
Give her words of affirmation.
Give her you.

A Love Relationship by Design

Purpose of a Cultivator

Ladies allow your men to cultivate, and men allow your woman to reciprocate. But, at the same time remember, he woman cannot reciprocate what the man does not cultivate. Simply stated, if the man does not sow into a woman, he cannot expect to reap anything from the woman. The cultivation process is specifically detailed to unique needs. Relationships are like plants, if they are not watered, they will wither and die. When a man sow into a woman, she will reciprocate those actions. In this process the man can bring the best out of that woman based his ability to give her what she needs, such as words of affirmation and etc.

A man who does not know his wife's family history may not be able to help her in the future. She can become a mystery to him or an issue of complexity. Cultivating a woman who grew up in a fully functioning home may be completely different than cultivating one who grew up with an absent father. She may require more attention because of a void left over from her early childhood. In a sense, a man may be required to show her extra love and attention, but her reciprocating process will be off the charts. There is probably nothing you can ask that she will not do. Other times, it requires patience and understanding to break down the walls of a

A Love Relationship by Design

person who has lost trust. This may be necessary to earn the trust of a good woman. When she arrives into your life, you will testify how virtuous this woman is, but the outcome of the relationship depends on the cultivating process. Relationships are not born but made. When we mature in our process understand not only our current value to each other but also what you can become. Cultivation is what happens before the harvest. It is the prerequisite to the harvest. This means something has to have for the relationship to prosper. I hope the use of the word, "cultivation," is understood in the proper context. In a relational context, every woman possesses a love language, and the man involved in a relationship with her must speak that language fluently in order to communicate clearly and from the other side women must understand what that man needs are as well. The man must seek to understand what he is cultivating and what requirements are necessary to fulfill this task. I view people as a puzzle with different shapes but, when placed in the correct order, they create a clear picture.

In a panoramic view of life, we are subject to many changes, many obstacles, but also many blessings. If we embrace the revisions of life and allow God to open our eyes of understanding, we will not have to concede to disappointment. These revisions will only be a vehicle that transitions our lives into greatness. God is concerned about our well-being and, if allowed, will intervene for our good. Relationships are vital and are

A Love Relationship by Design

the very substance of our human experience. We are connected to others in more ways than we can understand. We can either tear each other down or pick each other up, and we get to decide which we will do. Once we have learned how to conduct ourselves with each other, we then realize that there is much greater and more important work to be accomplished.

Everything we learn during the development and process of our journey to be more like Christ is meant to lead us to one thing... this one thing is called *purpose*. While my son and I sat and watched the movie, "Hugo," I was inspired by the words spoken. He said his father once told him that life is like one big machine and machines don't have spare parts. Therefore I must have a purpose.

God did not create spare people. Each and every person has a reason for their existence, although, it may be distinctively different. We crossed paths with other people to fulfill certain causes even if it only for a short periods. God can use anyone who chooses to fulfill a certain calling. God is phenomenal in His range and does not care about the past. He used a prostitute name Rehab to hide His spies; a young boy name David to slay the giant Goliath; and a radical persecutor of Christians name Saul, changed his name, and made him the most prolific preacher in building and directing the new testament church as well as one of the most prominent authors of the Bible. This series of paradoxes, along with many others throughout the Bible, proves that God can and will use anyone who is willing and some not so willing. God will choose anyone He desires to fulfill His purpose. This is validated by scripture that tells us…

1 Corinthian 1:27 (NKJV) *"But God has chosen the foolish things of the world to put to shame the wise, and God has chosen the weak things of the world to put to shame the things which are mighty…"*

A Love Relationship by Design

Identifying God's Purpose

When you use your God given talents and abilities, He will expand your territory sort like the parable of the talents. Purpose takes on a whole new meaning when feeding the hungry, clothing the naked and visiting the sick or those in prison. When obedient in God's will, we can change a society. Just the opposite, we can put others at risk when we fail to comply with God's purpose for our lives. If you feel you have a calling get busy fulfilling it. Others will be transformed when words are spoken; when songs are sang; when poetry is heard; when books are read; and when prayers are felt.

Sometimes, it is the smallest of deeds that make the greatest impact. The cultivation process requires different variables such as sowing, watering, fertilizing, hoeing, nurturing, and reaping. The more we use our gifts the more fluent we become. On the other hand, if we do not practice these variables, like crops, the elements of life will cause the gifts to wither and die. There are people who have died without their ministry ever being felt; inventions never being created; prayers never felt; businesses never built; songs never sang; and books never read. Some people never step out in faith but bury their gifts along with the hopes and dreams of others with them.

A Love Relationship by Design

After I had reached one of the lowest points of my life, my young son, who was about nine at the time, came to visit. I was so down; I let him in and then went to lie across my bed. My son then came into the room, placed his arms around me and whispered these simple words, "Dad I Love You." This may sound simple, but at that moment those words changed me. They gave me motivation to shake off my "feeling sorry for myself," because I realize I had a son to be an example for.

Another night as I wrestled with being alone and had so many questions for God, the tears began to roll down my face like a fountain. Like anyone else who has faced the aftermath of a divorce, I felt severely broken. I was so defeated; I asked God two things… "Do you really love me?" and "Are you pleased with my life?"

The next morning, as I was leaving for church, a good friend from my bible study called and spoke these life transforming words, "I don't know why I am calling you, but God dropped this into my spirit just now, He told me to tell you that, "HE LOVES YOU AND IS PLEASED WITH YOUR LIFE." My friend was being obedient to his purpose for that moment. He had no idea that I had prayed those exact words in prayer the night before but his fulfillment of purpose set me free. When you are led by the Holy Spirit, you may not know why you are doing what He asks of you, but the one receiving the message experiences a supernatural

A Love Relationship by Design

movement from God. Had my son not spoken those words, "I love you," and had my good friend not called and told me the words from God, I am not sure that I would not have just given up. I had friend's both male and female who just called and immediately started praying for me. I am grateful to have those friends. Just remember your obedience.

There are blessings that give birth out of you from your trials. It is beauty for ashes. What you lose is only to make way for the gain. I am not saying that God removes people to bring different people into your life, but God sometimes desires to bring your gifts to the surface. Often, the only way for you to use those gifts are through the trying of your faith. Treasures are discovered in places you have never gone and through experiences you have never encountered. If I had never been tested in this way, I would never had written and recorded two meaningful poetic CD's or written this book.

These items that I cherish were given birth from the storm. In the same manner, people who were laid off or fired from their jobs decided to start their own businesses and have never been happier. Further, those businesses become economic blessings to those people they hire. Remember, failure to utilize your gifts can and will affect the lives of others. Your gifts are someone else's opportunity.

A Love Relationship by Design

The Effect of Neglected Purpose

David is one of my favorite writers in the bible. He was a man after God's own heart but when he neglected his purpose for a day, the outcome proved destructive. When we neglect our purpose, sometimes, hope, encouragement, and direction can be altered. We can actually be in way from others coming to Christ. David behavior got another man killed and his pregnant. If he had simply lead his troops to battle as was the custom of the king, he would not have been at his palace to commit these acts.

Any time you focus on something that has the potential to conceive in your mind, it then gives birth to sin and sin to death. Now make note that had David lead the troops into the battle himself the outcome may have been different. David would not have lusted after Bathsheba and he would not have sinned by bringing her into his court and sending her lawful husband Uriah to his death on the frontlines of battle.

Lust, greed and pride can destroy ministries along with families. Four bad things resulted from David not fulfilling his kingly purpose; the look up; the hook up; the set up; and the cover up. In the lookup, David pulled a background check on Bathsheba finding

A Love Relationship by Design

she was married to one of his top military men. But David decided to disregard that information, and sent his men to deliver Bathsheba to his palace, the hook up. It is interesting to note, that some may blame Bathsheba thinking that she may have enticed him, but in her defense, how could she deny the king. Just like David, someone can desire something they cannot afford. They know they cannot afford it but they buy it anyway. Now, this debt hanging over there head becomes the detractor of their purpose. Then they become consumed with trying to figure out how they are going to pay their bills when they should be focused on fulfilling God's purpose for their life.

Here are some facts to consider. The first thing is David should not have been at home; secondly, Bathsheba understood that the King David possessed the power of life and death, so if she resisted, her life could have been taken. It can seem strange that when we are not doing what we should be doing, we end up doing what we shouldn't. Bathsheba ended up pregnant by King David and not by her husband Uriah. This almost sounds like reality TV but proves that one slip from purpose can be costly. Now David has to figure out a way to get her husband home to make him think that the baby is his… the cover up! The only problem is he did not fall for the many attempts of David coercion. David finally schemed to have Uriah sent to the front line to have him killed—the set up! This proves that a missed assignment can cost even to the point of taking an innocent life. This is an extreme situation but someone's salvation may be resting on your obedience.

We find a like scenario in the life of Jonah In Jonah's case, God assigned him to go to Nineveh but instead Jonah ran in the opposite direction to Joppa. The people he was called to minister to where people he really did not like. Jonah would rather they perish than for God to use him to save them. Everyone's life on the boat was in danger because of Jonah.

God sent a storm after Jonah and finally the men threw him overboard and you know the rest of the story. The central thought is that sometimes God will send you into places you would rather not go, to deal with people you really don't want deal with. But God knows what He is doing. God knows best. Do not let your past encounters with people keep you from reaching back and showing them the love of Christ. Remember, while we were yet sinners, Christ died for us. Christ fulfillment of purpose is the reason we live.

A Love Relationship by Design

Servants of Each Other

Mark 10:45 (NKJV) *"For even the Son of Man did not come to be served, but to serve, and to give His life a ransom for many."*

Matthew 23:11 (NKJV) *"But the greatest among you shall be your servant."*

Being a servant is not always a natural instinct, in fact for most people it is the greatest challenge. It is a selfless act disregarding your own needs and desires. Dwight Frederick, an excellent bible Sunday school teacher, told an interesting illustration about babies crying out to be served. They cry out saying feed me, change me, hold me, and nurse me. This behavior says our human nature warrants to be served contrary to giving a service. Some of these precursors are reinforced in early childhood development and into adulthood. A vast number of relationships experience symptoms of behavior that is directly related to our experiences. When learn to look at our needs early, and forget that the other person has needs also, but when you learn to serve, you learn to put others before yourself. When a couple learn to do this for each, they become selfless. Change does not just happen on its own, we have to do things that promote change. A change of thinking and action must be instituted in order for behavioral change to take place.

This is evident in our expectations of one another. A man who grew up being catered to by a woman has a tendency as a man of wanting to be taken care of by a woman. He will sit around doing nothing refusing to work and assist his mate around the house. If he does any of the house chores, he expects credit and praise for doing them when he should have been helping anyway. This is the same case of a well-kept woman. Spared and spoiled as a young child alters her ability to give back. Self-centeredness and contentiousness shuts down her ability to operate as God had designed. She possesses a distorted sense of femininity. Her ability to take, take, and take some more while not giving is a result of her believing that everyone owes her. To the man, he believes that her serving him is required, and in this case neither the man nor woman is representative of a good servant. Each wants to be served and neither believes it is their duty to serve.

Servitude should go both ways, and should not be based on coercion to obtain something from the other person. Serving needs to be a willing behavior and not something you are forced to do. Good servitude is something you are honored to freely do.

A Love Relationship by Design

I pray that, through this book, the passion of Christ has ignited a fire that will burn in your heart for your relationships and that you will learn to love with a renewed and refined interest. I hope that perception is not an obstacle, but that with your keen ability to communicate effectively it will revise the attitudes toward each other. I pray that you search outside the box and discover innovative ways to bridge your differences. This requires effort from both parties in a relationship, but with patience and persistence it's viable. Purpose is the reason we exist. This is the reason God allows us to cross paths of others. A major role for the woman is to assist the man in accomplishing more than he can on his own. Man, under the order of God, is to provide structure and to help govern the woman's emotions. This helps both to integrate their resources for kingdom building. Like a link in a chain, if that link is not completely connected, it compromises the strength and purpose of that chain. Revisions look at the cause of the defect and then find a way to correct it. Man and woman, in some ways, can be like the relationship between the Jews and Gentiles. They found it difficult to co-exist together, but realized it was possible with the power of the Holy Spirit.

Ephesians 3:14-19 (NKJV) *"For this reason I bow my knees to the Father of our Lord Jesus Christ, from whom the whole family in heaven and earth is*

A Love Relationship by Design

named, that He would grant you, according to the riches of His glory, to be strengthened with might through His Spirit in the inner man, that Christ may dwell in your hearts through faith; that you, being rooted and grounded in love, may be able to comprehend with all the saints what is the width and length and depth and height—to know the love of Christ which passes knowledge; that you may be filled with all the fullness of God. Now to Him who is able to do exceedingly abundantly above all that we ask or think, according to the power that works in us, to Him be glory in the church by Christ Jesus to all generations, forever and ever." Amen.

A Love Relationship by Design

Author Biography

Stephen B. Wright, was born and raised in New Roads, LA. Wright was licensed and ordained by his church to minister at the age of twenty-one.

A year later, Wright wrote his first letter to the church in Pointe Coupee Parish, LA, entitled the "*Revival Pages*" from the book of Chronicles 7:14. This short essay was the outgrowth of what he believed God had laid on his heart to promote prayer and unity.

"*A Love Relationship by Design*," is Wright's first published work. Written in laymen's terms, this is a handbook for couples to review and then to revise how they think, so that they can fully engage in their relationship designed the way God intended.

Footnotes:
[i] 1 Corinthians 11:3

www.ingramcontent.com/pod-product-compliance
Lightning Source LLC
Chambersburg PA
CBHW060726110426
42738CB00056B/1742